Microsoft®

Publisher 98

Illustrated Introductory

D1518797

Microsoft®
Publisher 98
Illustrated Introductory

Elizabeth Eisner Reding

COURSE
TECHNOLOGY

ONE MAIN STREET, CAMBRIDGE, MA 02142

an International Thomson Publishing company I(T)P®

Cambridge • Albany • Bonn • Boston • Cincinnati • London • Madrid • Melbourne • Mexico City
New York • Paris • San Francisco • Singapore • Tokyo • Toronto • Washington

Microsoft Publisher 98—Illustrated Introductory

is published by Course Technology

Managing Editor:	Nicole Jones Pinard
Product Manager/Developmental Editor:	Jennifer Thompson
Production Editor:	Daphne Barbas
Composition House:	GEX, Inc.
QA Manuscript Reviewers:	John Bosco, Jon Greacen, Alex White
Text Designer:	Joseph Lee
Cover Designer:	Joseph Lee

© 1999 by Course Technology — I(T)P®

For more information contact:

Course Technology
One Main Street
Cambridge, MA 02142

International Thomson Publishing Europe
Berkshire House 168-173
High Holborn
London WCIV 7AA
England

Thomas Nelson Australia
102 Dodds Street
South Melbourne, 3205
Victoria, Australia

Nelson Canada
1120 Birchmount Road
Scarborough, Ontario
Canada M1K 5G4

International Thomson Editores
Campos Eliseos 385, Piso 7
Col. Polanco
11560 Mexico D.F. Mexico

International Thomson Publishing GmbH
Königswinterer Strasse 418
53227 Bonn
Germany

International Thomson Publishing Asia
211 Henderson Road
#05-10 Henderson Building
Singapore 189969

International Thomson Publishing Japan
Hirakawacho Kyowa Building, 3F
2-2-1 Hirakawacho
Chiyoda-ku, Tokyo 102
Japan

Trademarks
Course Technology and the Open Book logo are registered trademarks of Course Technology.
Illustrated Projects and the Illustrated Series are trademarks of Course Technology.

I(T)P® The ITP logo is a registered trademark of International Thomson Publishing Inc.

Some of the product names and company names used in this book have been used for identification purposes only and may be trademarks or registered trademarks of their respective manufacturers and sellers.

Disclaimer
Course Technology reserves the right to revise this publication and make changes from time to time in its content without notice.

ISBN 0-7600-6106-8

Printed in Canada

10 9 8 7 6 5 4 3 2 1 WC 03 02 01 00 99

Exciting New Illustrated Products

The Illustrated Projects™ Series: The Quick, Visual Way to Apply Computer Skills

Looking for an inexpensive, easy way to supplement almost any application text and give your students the practice and tools they'll need to compete in today's competitive marketplace? Each text includes more than 50 real-world, useful projects—like creating a resume and setting up a loan worksheet—that let students hone their computer skills. These two-color texts have the same great two-page layout as the Illustrated Series.

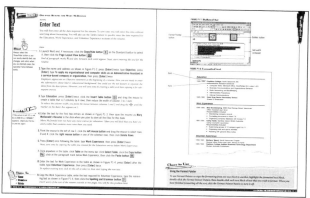

Illustrated Projects titles are available for the following:

- ▶ Microsoft Access
- ▶ Microsoft Excel
- ▶ Microsoft Office Professional
- ▶ Microsoft Publisher
- ▶ Microsoft Word

- ▶ Creating Web Sites
- ▶ World Wide Web
- ▶ Adobe PageMaker
- ▶ Corel WordPerfect

Illustrated Interactive® Series: The Safe, Simulated Way to Learn Computer Skills

The Illustrated Interactive Series uses multimedia technology to teach computer concepts and application skills. Students learn via a CD-ROM that simulates the actual software and provides a controlled learning environment in which every keystroke is monitored. Plus, all products in this series feature the same step-by-step instructions as the Illustrated Series. An accompanying workbook reinforces the skills that students learn on the CD.

Illustrated Interactive titles are available for the following applications:*

- ▶ Microsoft Windows 98
- ▶ Microsoft Office 97
- ▶ Microsoft Word 97
- ▶ Microsoft Excel 97

- ▶ Microsoft Access 97
- ▶ Microsoft PowerPoint 97
- ▶ Computer Concepts

Standalone & networked versions available. Runs on Windows 3.1, 95, and NT. CD-only version available for Computer Concepts and Office 97.

CourseKits™: Offering You the Freedom to Choose

Balance your course curriculum with Course Technology's mix-and-match approach to selecting texts. CourseKits provide you with the freedom to make choices from more than one series. When you choose any two or more Course Technology products for one course, we'll discount the price and package them together so your students pick up one convenient bundle at the bookstore.

Contact your sales representative to find out more about these Illustrated products.

Preface

Welcome to *Microsoft Publisher 98 – Illustrated Introductory*! This book in our highly visual new design offers new users a hands-on introduction to Microsoft Publisher 98 and also serves as an excellent reference for future use.

▶ Organization and Coverage

This text contains seven units that cover basic Microsoft Publisher 98 skills. In these units students learn how to plan and design a publication, format text, work with art, and create a publication using the Catalog. They also learn how to define and use styles, work with multiple pages, enhance a publication with special features, and create a Web page.

▶ About this Approach

What makes the Illustrated approach so effective at teaching software skills? It's quite simple. Each skill is presented on two facing pages, with the step-by-step instructions on the left page, and large screen illustrations on the right. Students can focus on a single skill without having to turn the page. This unique design makes information extremely accessible and easy to absorb, and provides a great reference for students after the course is over. This hands-on approach also makes it ideal for both self-paced or instructor-led classes. The modular structure of the book also allows for great flexibility; you can cover the units in any order you choose.

Each lesson, or "information display," contains the following elements:

Each two-page spread focuses on a single skill.

Concise text that introduces the basic principles in the lesson and integrates the brief case study.

Unit D — Publisher 98

Cropping an Image

Even though Publisher comes with thousands of images from which to choose, you may find that the art you've chosen needs some modification. Perhaps a picture's contents are not to your liking. In that case, you can always trim, or crop, portions of the artwork. A graphic image can be cropped vertically or horizontally—or both at the same time. Even though they are not visible, cropped portions of an image are still there—they are just concealed. Gary wants to crop portions of the sunset he has inserted on the second page.

Steps 1 2 3 4

1. Click the Next Page button ▶ on the horizontal scroll bar
   You want to zoom in on the artwork.

2. Click the image in the center panel of the page, then press [F9]
   Compare your page to Figure D-6. You want to crop the right side of the image so that the plant is concealed.

3. Click the Crop Picture button ⌗ on the Formatting toolbar, then place the Cropping pointer ⊹ over the center-right handle
   You drag the edge of the image so that the whole plant and all its components cannot be seen in the frame. The coordinates on the ruler are given as a guide: you should also look at the image as you trim it to be sure the correct parts are cropped.

   QuickTip
   To crop both edges simultaneously and equally, press and hold [Ctrl], then drag the ⊹ pointer.

4. Drag ⊹ to 5" H
   Next you crop the lower edge of the image. The Crop Picture button stays selected until you click it to turn it off, so you can continue cropping.

5. Place the pointer over the center-bottom handle, drag the ⊹ pointer up to 2¼" V, then click ⌗
   Now that the image is cropped, you want to resize it to scale.

6. Position the pointer over the bottom-right handle so that it changes to ↖, press and hold [Shift], then drag ↖ to the ruler guide at 2⅜" V
   Next, you reposition the image. You want the image to appear centered in the column.

   QuickTip
   Don't worry if you see misspelled words; they will be corrected later.

7. Position the pointer on the selected image so it changes to ⊕, then drag the selected image between 3¼" H and 6" H
   Compare your image to Figure D-7. Zoom out and save your work.

8. Press [F9], then click the Save button 🖫 on the Standard toolbar

▶ PUBLISHER D-6 **WORKING WITH ART**

Hints as well as trouble-shooting advice right where you need it — next to the step itself.

Clear step-by-step directions, with what students are to type in bold, explain how to complete the specific task.

Every lesson features large representations of what the screen should look like as students complete the numbered steps.

The innovative design draws the students' eyes to important areas of the screens.

Other Features

The two-page lesson format featured in this book provides the new user with a powerful learning experience. Additionally, this book contains the following features:

▶ **Real-World Case**
The case study used throughout the textbook, a fictitious advertising agency called Image Masters, is designed to be "real-world" in nature and introduces the kinds of activities that students will encounter when working with Microsoft Publisher 98. With a real-world case, the process of solving problems will be more meaningful to students.

▶ **End of Unit Material**
Each unit concludes with a Concepts Review that tests students' understanding of what they learned in the unit. A Skills Review follows the Concepts Review and provides students with additional hands-on practice of the skills they learned in the unit. The Skills Review is followed by Independent Challenges, which pose case problems for students to solve. At least one Independent Challenge in each unit asks students to use the World Wide Web to solve the problem as indicated by a Web Work icon. The Visual Workshop that follows the Independent Challenges helps students to develop critical thinking skills. Students are shown completed documents and are asked to recreate them from scratch.

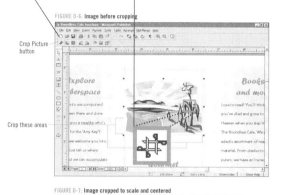

FIGURE D-6: Image before cropping

FIGURE D-7: Image cropped to scale and centered

Recoloring an object

In addition to being cropped, images can be altered through recoloring. Once an object has been selected, right-click it, click Change Object, then click Recolor Object (or click Format on the menu bar, then Recolor Object). This method lets you change all the colors in the picture to different shades of a single color—ideal when creating a watermark effect. Figure D-8 shows the Recolor Object dialog box.

FIGURE D-8: Recolor Object dialog box

Click here for additional colors

Sample image displays here

Click to restore the original colors

WORKING WITH ART   PUBLISHER D-7 ◀

Clues to Use Boxes provide concise information that either expands on the major lesson skill or describes an independent task that in some way relates to the major lesson skill.

The page numbers are designed like a road map. PUBLISHER indicates that it's a Publisher unit, D indicates Unit D, and 7 indicates the page within the unit. This map allows for the greatest flexibility in content – each unit stands completely on its own.

Instructor's Resource Kit

The Instructor's Resource Kit is Course Technology's way of putting the resources and information needed to teach and learn effectively into your hands. With an integrated array of teaching and learning tools that offer you and your students a broad range of technology-based instructional options, we believe this kit represents the highest quality and most cutting-edge resources available to instructors today. To obtain these resources, visit the Instructor Resources page for this book at www.course.com, or contact our Customer Service department. The resources available with this book are:

Course Test Manager Designed by Course Technology, this cutting-edge Windows-based testing software helps instructors design, administer, and print tests at the compter and have their exams automatically graded.

Instructor's Manual Quality assurance tested, the Instructor's Manual includes:
- Solutions to all lessons and end-of-unit material
- Detailed lecture topics for each unit with teaching tips
- Extra Independent Challenges
- Task References
- Transparency Masters

WWW.COURSE.COM We encourage students and instructors to visit our Web site at www.course.com to find articles about current teaching and software trends, featured texts, interviews with authors, demos of Course Technology's software, Frequently Asked Questions about our products, and much more. This site is also where you can gain access to the Faculty Online Companion or Student Online Companion for this text — see below for more information.

Course Faculty Online Companion Available at www.course.com, this World Wide Web site offers Course Technology customers a password-protected Instructor Resources page where you can find everything you need to prepare for class, including the Instructor's Manual in an electronic Portable Document Format (PDF) file and Adobe Acrobat Reader software. Periodically updated items include any updates and revisions to the text and Instructor's Manual, links to other Web sites, and access to student and solution files. This site will continue to evolve throughout the semester. Contact your Customer Service Representative for the site address and password.

Course Student Online Companion Available at www.course.com, this book features its own Student Online Companion where students can go to gain access to Web sites that will help them complete the Web Work Independent Challenges. These links are updated on a regular basis. This site will continue to evolve throughout the semester.

Student Files To use this book students must have the Student Files. See the inside front or inside back cover for more information on the Student Files. Adopters of this text are granted the right to post the Student Files on any stand-alone computer or network.

Brief Contents

Contents

 ► │ Publisher 98 │

Getting Started with Microsoft Publisher 98

Creating a Publication

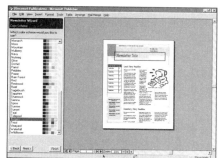

Contents

Formatting Text

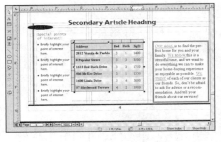

Working with Art

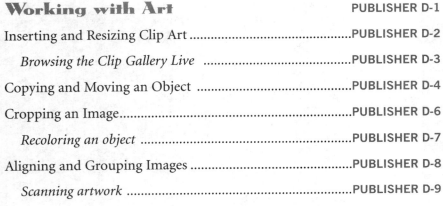

Enhancing a Publication

Contents

Using Special Features

PUBLISHER G-1

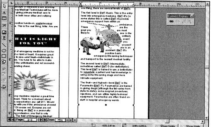

Credits

Figures E-5, E-6, E-7, E-13, E-14, E-18, E-23, E-24
From Titanic: Adventure out of Time, courtesy of CyberFlix, Inc.

Figures E-16, E-22, E-25
Left page, and lower left of right page, courtesy of Corbis-Bettmann; Upper and middle right of right page, from Titanic: Adventure out of Time, courtesy of CyberFlix, Inc.

Figure E-19
Courtesy of Corbis-Bettmann

Unit A

Getting
Started with Microsoft Publisher 98

Objectives

- ► Define publication software
- ► Start Publisher 98
- ► View the Publisher window
- ► Open and save a publication
- ► Enter text in a frame
- ► View and print a publication
- ► Get Help
- ► Close a publication and exit Publisher

Microsoft Publisher 98 is a popular desktop publishing program that operates using the Windows operating system. In this unit, you will learn how to start Publisher and use elements found in the Publisher window and menus. You will also learn how to open and save existing files, enter text in a publication, view and print a publication, and use the extensive online Help system. ◄━━━ Carlos Mendoza is an account executive at Image Masters, a small advertising agency. Carlos will use Publisher to create a flyer announcing the location of its new office.

Publisher 98

Defining Publication Software

Publisher is a desktop publishing program. A **desktop publishing** program lets you combine text and graphics, as well as worksheets and charts you may have created in other programs, to produce a document. A document created in Publisher is called a **publication**. Table A-1 lists examples of the types of publications you can create. Carlos loves using Publisher because he can create a variety of professional-looking publications quickly and easily. The benefits of using Publisher include the ability to:

Create professional publications
With Publisher, Carlos can create a variety of publications quickly and easily. Publisher comes with a Catalog that lets him choose the type of publication he wants to design, helps him decide on its appearance, and then suggests a possible placement of text and graphics to complete the publication.

Use clip art
A picture is worth a thousand words. Artwork not only makes any publication appear more vibrant and interesting, but also helps explain your ideas. Publisher comes with more than 10,000 pieces of artwork. Any of these illustrations, photographs, and decorative elements can be incorporated into your publications. In addition, any other personal illustrations and photographs can be electronically imported into the **Clip Gallery**, the online artwork organizer, with the use of a scanner. Carlos often adds artwork to enhance his publications and add emphasis.

Create logos
Most organizations want a special symbol, shape, or color—or combination of these—to attach a recognizable visual to their name. This distinctive shape, called a **logo**, can be created using Publisher's Logo Wizard or by creating any artwork and text. Figure A-1 illustrates a sample flyer that contains clip art and text combined to form a logo. Carlos is often asked to create such logos for clients.

Make your work look consistent
Publisher has many tools to help you create consistent publications that have similar design elements. Carlos might, for example, want to have an information box in the lower-left corner on the back page of all Image Masters flyers. Using rulers and layout guides, he can create grids that are visible only on the screen to help him position graphics and text on a page. Once this framework is complete, he can save this publication as a **template**, a special publication that serves as a master and can be used to create another publication.

Work with multiple pages
Publisher makes it easy to work with multipage publications. Pages can be added and deleted as necessary and can be moved within a publication. Text can be imported from a word processor or created in Publisher. Text that continues on more than one page is connected and flows logically between pages. Carlos likes to start an interesting article on one page and then continue it on another.

Emphasize special text
A publication looks boring if all the text looks the same. Using different fonts and sizes, Carlos makes the text look more interesting. Text styles also express different meanings and help convey the messages. He uses **pull quotes**, which set a short statement off to the side, to grab a reader's attention and **sidebars** to make important text stand out.

Publish on the Internet
Because the Internet is a vital tool to businesses, Publisher can be used to create World Wide Web pages using the Web Site Wizard. Carlos is often asked to incorporate design elements, such as a corporate logo, into a Web page. The Web Site Wizard makes it easy to include links and graphics.

FIGURE A-1: **Sample flyer**

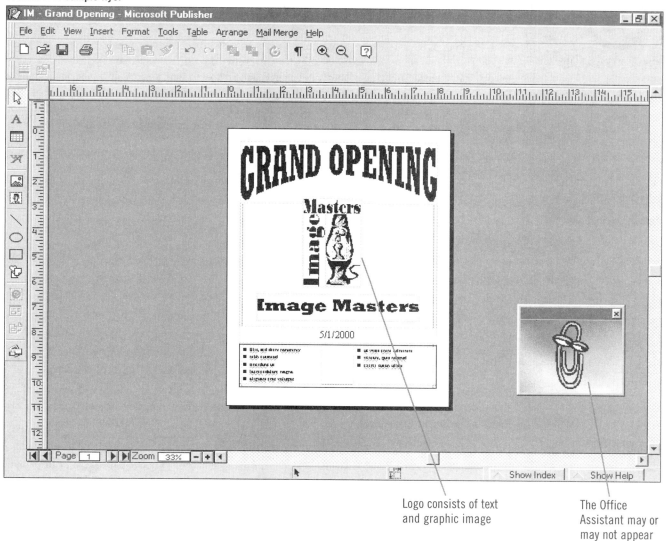

Logo consists of text and graphic image

The Office Assistant may or may not appear

TABLE A-1: **Common publications**

publication	examples
Periodical	Newsletters, booklets
Promotional	Advertisements, flyers, press releases
Informational	Brochures, signs, calendars, forms
Stationery	Letterhead, labels, business cards, envelopes, postcards
Specialty	Banners, airplanes, origami, resumes

Publisher 98

Starting Publisher 98

To start Publisher, you use the Start button on the taskbar. Click Programs, then click the Microsoft Publisher program icon. A slightly different procedure might be required for computers on a network and those that use utility programs to enhance Windows. If you need assistance, ask your instructor or technical support person for help. When you start Publisher, the computer displays the Catalog. This dialog box lets you select a Wizard, an existing publication, or a blank page. Carlos begins by starting Publisher, and he opens a blank full-page publication.

1. **Locate the Start button on the taskbar**
   The Start button is on the left side of the taskbar and is used to start programs on your computer.

QuickTip

Microsoft Publisher 98 can be used with either Windows 98 or Windows 95.

2. **Click the Start button**
   Microsoft Publisher is located in the Programs group, located at the top of the Start menu, as shown in Figure A-2.

3. **Point to Programs**
   All the programs, or applications, installed on your computer can be found in this area of the Start menu. You can see the Microsoft Publisher icon and other Microsoft programs, as shown in Figure A-3. Your Programs menu might look different depending on the programs installed on your computer.

Trouble?

If you don't see the Microsoft Publisher 98 icon, look in a folder called Microsoft Office or Office 97.

4. **Click the Microsoft Publisher program icon** 📖
   Publisher opens and the Catalog dialog box opens. This dialog box has four tabs: Publications by Wizard, Publications by Design, Blank Publications, and Existing Publications. You decide to open a blank full-page publication.

5. **Click the Blank Publications tab, click Full Page if necessary, then click Create**
   A blank full-page publication displays on the screen. In the next lesson, you will familiarize yourself with the elements of the Publisher window.

FIGURE A-2: **Start menu**

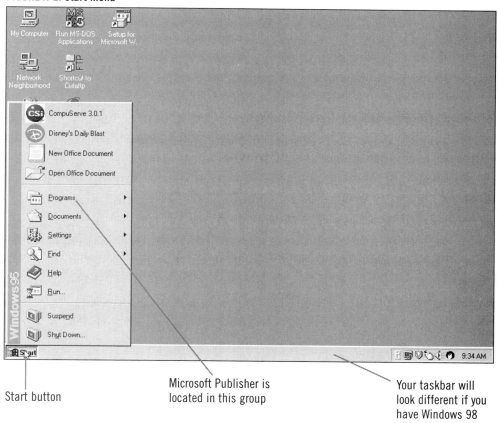

Start button

Microsoft Publisher is
located in this group

Your taskbar will
look different if you
have Windows 98

FIGURE A-3: **Programs available on your computer**

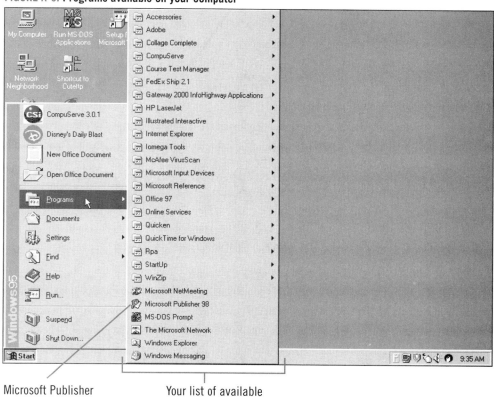

Microsoft Publisher
program icon

Your list of available
programs might vary

Viewing the Publisher Window

The area where a new or existing publication appears is called the **workspace**. The workspace is where you actually work on a publication. All the pages within a publication are visible here. Unlike most other programs, in Publisher only one publication can be open at a time. ━━━ Carlos takes some time to familiarize himself with the Publisher workspace and its elements before he works on the flyer. Compare the descriptions below to Figure A-4.

Details

 The **title bar** displays the program name (Microsoft Publisher) and the filename of the open worksheet (in this case, Unsaved Publication because the file has not yet been named and saved). The title bar also contains a control menu box, a Close button, and resizing buttons.

 The **menu bar** contains menus from which you choose Publisher commands. As with all Windows programs, you can choose a menu command by clicking it with the mouse or by pressing [Alt] plus the underlined letter in the menu name.

 The **toolbars** contain buttons for the most frequently used Publisher commands. The **Standard toolbar** is located just below the menu bar and contains buttons corresponding to the most frequently used Publisher features. Place the pointer over each button to display the ScreenTip to see what each button does. To choose a button, simply click it with the left mouse button. The face of any button has a graphic representation of its function; for instance, the Print button has a printer on its face.

Trouble?

Your rulers may have different beginning and ending numbers depending on the size of your monitor, the resolution of your display, and the positioning of the page on the workspace.

 Horizontal and vertical **rulers** display beneath the toolbars and to the left of the workspace. Rulers help you precisely measure the size of objects as well as place objects in precise locations on a page. These rulers also can be moved from the edge of the workspace to a more convenient position on the page.

 The **workspace page** contains the currently displayed page.

 Page navigation buttons below the workspace let you move from page to page either by typing the page number you want in the Change Page text box or by clicking the **First page**, **Previous page**, **Next page**, or **Last page button**.

 Click the **Select Zoom Mode button** to make the page larger or smaller, or click the **Zoom In** or **Zoom Out buttons** to change the size of the current page.

 The **status bar** is located at the bottom of the Publisher window. The left side of the status bar provides a brief description of the active command or task in progress. The center of the status bar shows the object status, which includes the size and position of selected objects. The right side of the status bar lets you access Publisher's Help system.

 The **scratch area** surrounds the publication page and can be used to store objects.

FIGURE A-4: **Blank Publication**

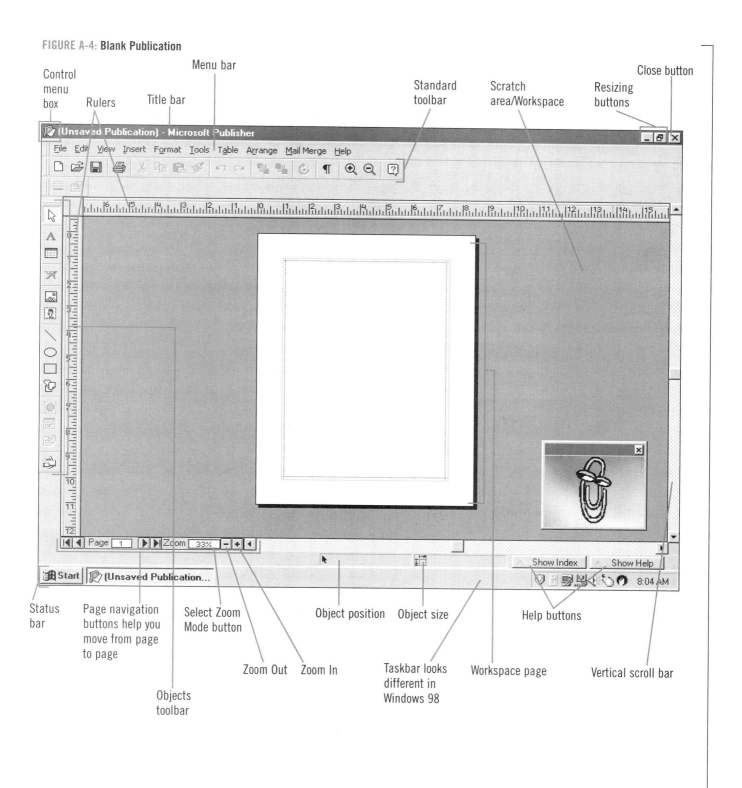

Control menu box

Rulers

Title bar

Menu bar

Standard toolbar

Scratch area/Workspace

Resizing buttons

Close button

Status bar

Page navigation buttons help you move from page to page

Objects toolbar

Select Zoom Mode button

Zoom Out

Zoom In

Object position

Object size

Taskbar looks different in Windows 98

Workspace page

Help buttons

Vertical scroll bar

Publisher 98

Opening and Saving a Publication

Often a project is completed in stages: you might start working on a publication and then stop to do other work or take a break. Later, you'll resume working and complete it. Sometimes it's more efficient to create a new publication by modifying one that already exists. This approach saves you from having to re-create existing information. Throughout this book, you will be instructed to open a file from your Project Disk, use the Save As command to create a copy of the file with a new name, and then modify the new file by following the lesson steps. Saving the files with new names keeps your original Project Disk files intact in case you have to start the lesson over again or you wish to repeat an exercise. You can slightly enlarge your publication by hiding the Windows taskbar. ✎ Carlos started the Image Masters flyer and is ready to finish it. Follow along as Carlos opens the Image Masters flyer, then uses the Save As command to create a copy of the file with a new name.

QuickTip

To hide the taskbar, click the Start button, point to Settings, click Taskbar, click the Auto hide check box on the Taskbar Options tab, then click OK.

1. Click the Open button 🗁 on the Standard toolbar
The Open Publication dialog box opens. See Figure A-5.

2. Click the Look in list arrow
A list of the available drives appears. Locate the drive that contains your Project Disk. In these lessons we assume your Project Disk is in drive A.

3. Click 3½ Floppy (A:)
A list of the files on your Project Disk appears.

4. Click the file PUB A-1, notice that the Preview pane shows a reduced image of the selected publication, then click Open
The file PUB A-1 opens. You could also double-click the filename to open the file. To create and save a copy of this file with a new name, you use the Save As command.

Trouble?

Publisher may display a message that the printer cannot be initialized. Click OK to change to your default printer.

5. Click File on the menu bar, then click Save As
The Save As dialog box opens.

6. Make sure the Save in list box displays the drive containing your Project Disk and that the Save Preview check box is checked
You should save all your files to your Project Disk, unless instructed otherwise.

7. Select the current filename in the File name text box, if necessary, then type Grand Opening flyer
See Figure A-6.

QuickTip

Use the Save As command to create a new publication from an existing one. Use the Save command to store any changes made to an existing file on your disk.

8. Click Save
The Save As dialog box closes, the file PUB A-1 closes, and a duplicate file named Grand Opening flyer is now open, as shown in Figure A-7. To save the publication in the future, you can click File on the menu bar, then click Save, or click the Save button on the Standard toolbar.

FIGURE A-5: **Open Publication dialog box**

Available files and folders display here

The selected filename will appear here

Click to display a list of available drives

A preview of the selected file displays here

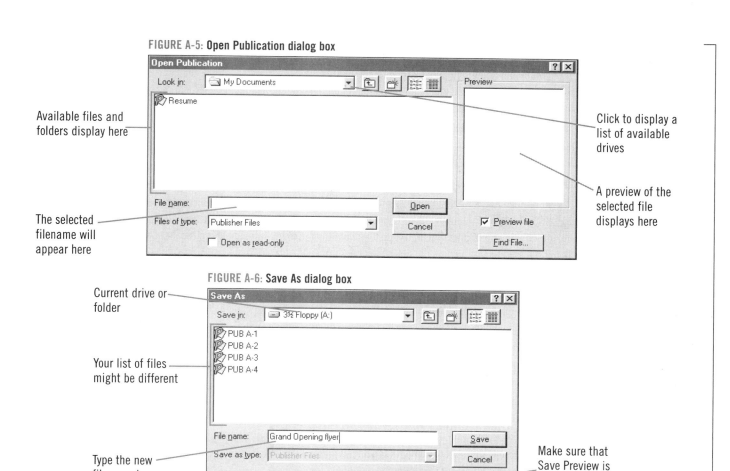

FIGURE A-6: **Save As dialog box**

Current drive or folder

Your list of files might be different

Type the new filename here

Make sure that Save Preview is selected

FIGURE A-7: **Grand Opening flyer publication**

Publication name displays in the title bar

Publisher 98

Entering Text in a Frame

In word processing, text is entered directly on a page. In desktop publishing, however, text is only a small part of a publication. Graphic objects are also used. Rather than enter text next to a margin, text in a publication is created in a text frame. A **text frame** is a graphic object in which text is typed. A frame can be moved, resized, and connected to other frames. A graphic object can be selected by clicking anywhere within it. When selected, small (usually black) squares called **handles** display around the perimeter. A frame can contain text, graphics, tables, and other frames. ✎ Carlos enters some additional text needed within the flyer.

Steps 1234

Trouble?

Periodically, a dialog box may appear suggesting that you save your work. Click Yes to save your publication; click No to save your work at a later time.

1. **Click the Text Frame Tool [A] on the Object toolbar to create the text frame**
   The Formatting toolbar appears and the pointer changes to +. You want to create a rectangular text frame that is slightly smaller than the Image Masters logo and located to its right in the publication. You use the object coordinates to precisely size and position the object.

2. **Position the + pointer so that the object location is at 3.5, 3.25 inches, then drag to create a rectangle whose object size is 3.75 × 2.75 inches**
   As you drag the object shape, the coordinates on the status bar change to display the object size and position of the pointer in the workspace. The text frame displays as shown in Figure A-8. When the mouse button is released, the text frame appears as a selected object, surrounded by handles, with the insertion point blinking at the top-left corner. This means that it is ready for you to type text. Before typing the text, however, you decide to use the Zoom feature to make the text readable. You can zoom in and out of a page using the View menu, the Zoom In/Zoom Out buttons on the status bar, or the [F9] keyboard shortcut. When text is too small to be legible, it is called greeked. The **greeking** text is automatically on in Publisher and displays small text as a series of x's.

QuickTip

Placeholders (sometimes in Latin text) are often used in publications as reminders of where information should be inserted.

3. **Press [F9], type We are very excited about our new office space. Here, we will be able to offer you services in a more professional atmosphere. Please join us at our Grand Opening celebration on Thursday, October 1, 2000., press [Enter] twice, then type Our new address is Crimson Corner,, press [Enter], then type Suite 200, Santa Fe, NM 87501**
   Now you enlarge the text to make it easier to read. **Point size** is the height of a character, measured in points. The text is currently at 10 point; try changing it to 16 point.

4. **Drag the I pointer to select all the text in the frame, click the Font Size list arrow [10 ▾] on the Formatting toolbar, then click 16**
   The text in the text frame is shown in Figure A-9. You decide you want to see as much of the publication as possible without greeking the text frame.

Trouble?

The zoom level is determined by the size of the object selected at the time you press [F9].

5. **Click the Select Zoom Mode button, click 50%, then click anywhere on the scratch area to deselect the text frame**
   Although you have more entries to make, you save your work and plan on completing the flyer later.

6. **Click the Save button [💾] on the Standard toolbar**
   It is a good idea to save your work early and often in the creation process, especially before making significant changes to the publication or before printing.

FIGURE A-8: **Text frame in publication**

Formatting toolbar

Text Frame Tool

Object toolbar

Text frame

Handles

Greeked text

Object coordinates for position of selected text frame

Object coordinates for size of selected text frame

FIGURE A-9: **Completed text in text frame**

Indicates current Zoom level

Select Zoom Mode button

We are very excited about our new office space. Here, we will be able to offer you services in a more professional atmosphere. Please join us at our Grand Opening celebration on Thursday, October 1, 2000.

Our new address is Crimson Corner, Suite 200, Santa Fe, NM 87501

Text frame outline doesn't appear when printed

CLUES TO USE

Understanding frames

Frames are used to contain text, pictures (graphic images), or tables. Any frame can be resized or moved, and can also be used in layers. In addition, framed text can be wrapped around a framed object. The advantage to using frames is that any contents in the frame can be moved anywhere within a publication. Unlike in word processing, where all text and graphics are placed relative to margins, frames can be moved wherever you want in whatever size you choose. Figure A-10 shows text wrapped around a framed graphic image.

FIGURE A-10: **Text wrapped around a picture**

Viewing and Printing a Publication

When a publication is completed, you can print it to have a paper copy to reference, file, or send to others. You can also print a publication that is not complete to review it or work on when you are not at a computer. Before you print a publication, it is good to preview it using the Zoom feature to make sure that it will fit on a page the way you want. Table A-2 provides printing tips. Carlos prints a copy of the Image Masters flyer to show to a co-worker.

Trouble?

If a file is sent to print and the printer is off, an error message appears.

1. **Make sure the printer is on and contains paper**
   You use Zoom Out to check the flyer's overall appearance.

2. **Click the Zoom Out button ⊟ on the horizontal scroll bar once**
   You could also click the Select Zoom Mode button, then click 33% or Full Page. The page displays within the workspace window, as shown in Figure A-11. If there were multiple pages, you would see only one page. To see additional pages, you can click Next Page or Previous Page.

3. **Click the Save button 🖫**
   Now that the publication is saved, you can print it.

QuickTip

You can also use the Print button on the Standard toolbar 🖨 to print every page in a publication.

4. **Click File on the menu bar, then click Print**
   The Print dialog box opens, as shown in Figure A-12.

5. **Make sure that the Use Print Troubleshooter check box is not checked, that the All option button is selected, and that 1 appears in the Number of copies text box**
   Now you are ready to print the publication.

6. **Click OK**
   Review the publication to see if it printed as expected.

FIGURE A-11: Whole page in workspace

Next Page button

Previous Page button

Zoom Out button

FIGURE A-12: Print dialog box

Click here to select the printer

Set the number of copies here

Print Troubleshooter should not be checked

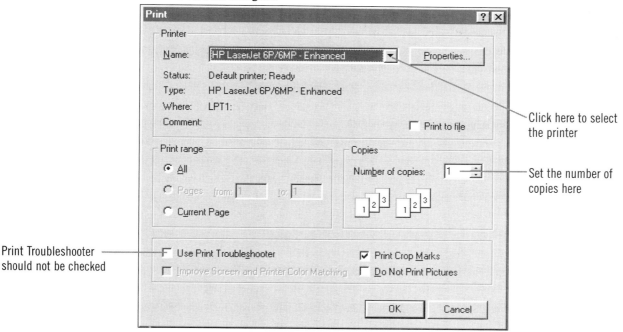

TABLE A-2: Publication printing tips

before you print	recommendation
Check the printer	Make sure that the printer is turned on and online, that it has paper, and that there are no error messages or warning signals
Check the printer selection	Use the Printer Name command in the Print dialog box to make sure the correct printer is selected

Publisher 98

Getting Help

Publisher features an extensive online Help system that gives you immediate access to definitions, explanations, and useful tips. The Help system displays along the right side of the workspace. When open, it can be viewed by using either the Index or Contents, or both. In addition, it can remain on the screen, allowing you to consult it as you work. The Index area lists information contained in Help; the displayed Contents reflects the selected Index item. You can turn the Index and Contents features on and off with the buttons on the status bar. ◢━━ Carlos decides to use Help to find out about wizards. First, because it may block the Help windows, he closes the Office Assistant.

1. **If necessary, click the Office Assistant Close button**
   Help information can be accessed at any time that Publisher is open.

Trouble?

The Contents side of your Help window may look different depending on the Help window that was displayed previously.

2. **Click the Show Index button** `⌃ Show Index` **on the status bar**
   The Index and Contents Help windows open, as shown in Figure A-13.
   You want information on Publisher 98 wizards. Because the Contents section matches your keystrokes, it's not usually necessary to type the entire word you're looking for.

3. **Type wiz, then click help with new publications**
   See Figure A-14. As you type characters, the Help index looks for entries that match your keystrokes and shows you possible matches. The Contents side automatically displays descriptions of the Index selection. You decide to read more about using wizards to create new publications.

Trouble?

If a yellow Help bubble appears, you can close it after reading it by pressing [Esc].

4. **Use the scroll bar to read the entire text in the How To tab in the Contents window**
   You decide to read the More Info tab to find out more.

5. **Click the More Info tab**
   You can read about creating publications not found in the wizards list.

6. **Click I don't see the type of publication I want, read the information in the dialog box, then click Done**
   Now that you are finished using Help, you can close the Index and Help windows.

7. **Click the Hide Help button** `▼ Hide Help` **on the status bar**
   Both Help windows close.

FIGURE A-13: Initial Help Index window

Type the subject for which you're searching here

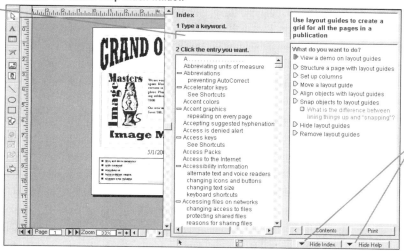

Buttons switch between Show and Hide depending on whether Help is open or closed

FIGURE A-14: PageWizard information in Index and Contents windows

Read information found within both tabs

Select the topic on which you want information

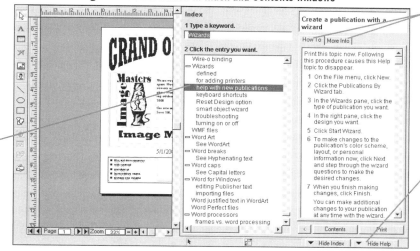

Click to close the Index and Contents windows

Using the Office Assistant

The Office Assistant provides helpful tips and information at the click of your mouse. To turn it on, click ⌨ on the Standard toolbar. To turn it off, click the Office Assistant Close button. The default Microsoft Office Assistant is Clippit, although you can change its appearance by right-clicking its image and then clicking Choose Assistant. Once it is open, you can query the Office Assistant by clicking anywhere within its window. Figure A-15 shows the result of clicking the Office Assistant. Like Help's Contents window, the question that initially appears in the Office Assistant may vary, depending on what was previously displayed.

FIGURE A-15: Office Assistant dialog box

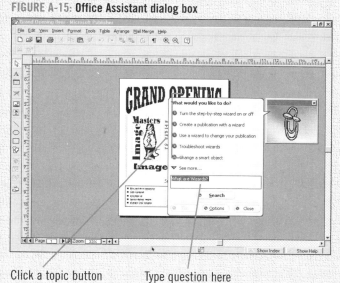

Click a topic button   Type question here

Publisher 98

Closing a Publication and Exiting Publisher

When you have finished working on a publication, you need to save the file and close it. Once you have saved a file and are ready to close it, click Close on the File menu. When you have completed all your work in Publisher, you need to exit the program. To exit Publisher, click Exit on the File menu. Closing a file puts away a publication file but leaves Publisher running. Exiting puts away a publication file and returns you to the desktop, where you can choose to run another program. ▶️ Carlos has finished adding the information to the Image Masters flyer and needs to attend a meeting, so he closes the publication and then exits Publisher.

1. **Click File on the menu bar**
   The File menu opens. See Figure A-16.

2. **Click Close**
   You could also click the Close button on the title bar instead of choosing File, Close Publication.

3. **If asked if you want to save your work, click Yes**
   Publisher closes the publication and displays a blank publication.

4. **Click File, then click Exit**
   You could also double-click the program control menu box to exit the program. Publisher closes and computer memory is freed up for other computing tasks.

FIGURE A-16: **Closing a publication using the File menu**

Program control menu box

Close command

Close window button

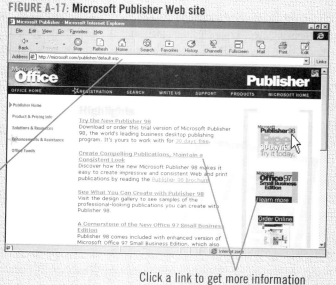

Exit command

Microsoft Publisher World Wide Web site

You can get even more information by accessing the Microsoft Publisher Web site. This constantly changing site offers tips and how-to information, as well as new developments. By clicking on the blue links, you can find additional information on this product. Figure A-17 shows the Publisher Web site, although it may look different on your screen because it changes so often. To find even more information, you can search the Internet (using a search engine such as Yahoo!) for any sites about Microsoft Publisher.

FIGURE A-17: **Microsoft Publisher Web site**

Site address

Click a link to get more information

Practice

▶ Concepts Review

Label each of the elements of the Publisher window shown in Figure A-18.

SAVE 1

OPEN FILE 2

TEXT FRAME TOOL 3

LETS you DRAG FRAME Handle 4

FIGURE A-18

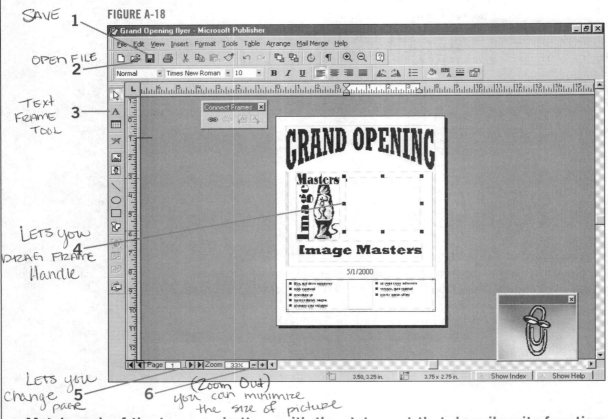

LETS you change page 5

6 *(Zoom Out) you can minimize the size of picture*

Match each of the terms or buttons with the statement that describes its function.

7. Used to save a publication on a disk B

8. Small black squares surrounding an object E

9. Provides a brief description of the active command F

10. Contains typed text C

11. Opens an existing publication A

12. Prints every page in the publication D

a. 🗁

b. 💾

c. Text frame

d. 🖨

e. Handles

f. Status bar

Select the best answer from the list of choices.

13. A document created in Publisher is called a:
a. Magazine.
b. Notebook.
c. Publication.
d. Brochure.

14. Which of the following statements about frames is false?
a. They can be moved.
b. They can be resized.
c. They can be inverted.
d. They can be connected to other frames.

15. Which key is pressed to zoom into a selected area?
a. [F8]
b. [F2]
c. [F6]
d. [F9]

16. A template is:
a. A special publication that serves as a master for other publications.
b. A short statement placed off to the side to grab a reader's attention.
c. An online artwork organizer.
d. A distinctive shape in a publication.

17. Greeked text displays as a series of:
a. y's.
b. x's.
c. z's.
d. t's.

18. Which button is used to create a text box?

a.

b. ⊠

c. A

d. 🖺

19. Which feature is used to enlarge a page?

a. Magnify

b. Enlarge

c. Amplify

d. Zoom In

20. Each of the following is found in the status bar, *except:*

a. Descriptions of commands and tasks.

b. The name of the current publication.

c. The Show Index button.

d. A selected object's size.

▶ Skills Review

1. Start Publisher and identify the elements in the publication window.
   a. Start Publisher.
   b. Open a blank full page.
   c. Try to identify as many elements in the Publisher window as you can without referring to the unit material.

2. Open and save an existing publication.
   a. Open the file PUB A-2. If you get a message to initialize the default printer, click OK.
   b. Save the publication as My Business Card.

3. Enter text in a frame.
   a. Create a text frame for your name, using Figure A-19 as a guide. (Substitute your own name.) Use a 16 point text size.
   b. Create a text frame for your address, using Figure A-19 as a guide. (Substitute your own address.) Use a 14 point text size.
   c. Save the publication.

4. View and print a publication.
   a. Zoom out as necessary to see the text in your publication greeked.
   b. Zoom in until all text is readable.
   c. Print one copy of the publication.

FIGURE A-19

5. Get Help.
    a. Click the Show Index button on the status bar.
    b. Find information on the Zoom feature.
    c. Print information in the Contents window.
    d. Close the Help window.

6. Close a publication and exit Publisher.
    a. Close your publication.
    b. Exit Publisher.

▶ Independent Challenges

1. Publisher's online Help provides definitions, explanations, procedures, and other helpful information. It also provides examples and demonstrations to show how Publisher features work. Topics include elements such as the workspace, frames, and selecting objects, as well as detailed information about Publisher commands and options. From an existing publication, explore Help by clicking the Show Index button. Find out about opening and saving a publication. (*Hint:* You may have to find information on more than one topic.) Print out the information.

2. Desktop publishing programs can be used to create many types of publications. Some examples of how Publisher can be used are discussed in the beginning of this unit. Use your own personal or business experiences to come up with five examples of how Publisher could be used in a business setting.

To complete this independent challenge:

a. Think of five business tasks that you could complete more efficiently by using a Publisher publication.
b. Sketch a sample of each publication.
c. Explain why Publisher is a better program to use for this publication than a word processor.
d. Type up your answers and print them out.

3. The Dirty Birds Cleaning Service (specializing in cleaning offices and individual homes) has hired you to design a flyer for its business. You've already gotten a head start on the flyer, but you need to add some text.

To complete this independent challenge:

a. Start Publisher if necessary, then open the file PUB A-3 and save it as Dirty Birds.
b. Add text that tells the types of services this cleaning service offers, including your fees.
c. Print the finished product.
d. Save your work.
e. Close the publication.

4. The World Wide Web has many sites for individuals and businesses. Imagine that you are going to start your own desktop publishing business. Explore the Web and examine home pages for other companies. List the features you think should be included in your page and make a sketch of how your page might look.

To complete this independent challenge:

a. Start Publisher if necessary, then open a new blank full-page publication.
b. Decide what features you want your ideal home page to have, and list these features.
c. Log on to the Internet and use any search engine (such as Yahoo!) to find sites for desktop publishing companies.
d. Sketch a design for your company's home page.
e. Sketch a logo for your company.

▶ Visual Workshop

Open the publication PUB A-4 on your Project Disk and add the text shown in Figure A-20, using the skills you learned in this unit. The font size in the text frame is 12 point. Save the publication as Happy Teeth Reminder on your Project Disk. Print the publication.

FIGURE A-20

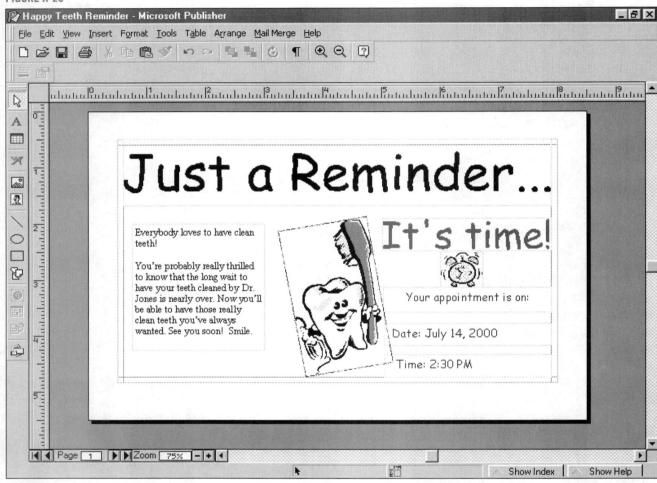

Creating
a Publication

- ▶ **Plan and design a publication**
- ▶ **Create a publication with the Catalog**
- ▶ **Replace frame text**
- ▶ **Add a graphic image**
- ▶ **Add a sidebar**
- ▶ **Add a pull quote**
- ▶ **Use the Design Gallery**
- ▶ **Group objects**

Now that you are familiar with the Publisher workspace and understand how to open and save a file, you are ready to create your own publication. You will learn how to use the Catalog to create a new publication. You will replace existing text and add a graphic image to the publication. ✎ Marjorie Raynovich, an intern at Image Masters, is learning how to use Publisher. She is on the newsletter team and is working on the latest issue.

Planning and Designing a Publication

Before you start a publication, you have to plan and design it. Planning involves knowing what information to include and identifying who will be reading it. Knowing the content and your audience helps you decide how the publication should look. Marjorie's first assignment is to create a one-page newsletter. She wants the newsletter to catch the eye of her readers. She includes the company logo (which is in electronic form) to identify the newsletter as Image Masters' and calls attention to specific text she wants to be sure is seen and understood.

Determine the purpose of the publication
Publisher lets you create a wide variety of publications using the Catalog. The subject matter is critical in determining the style and layout. By answering a few simple questions, Marjorie can create the appropriate type of publications for any task.

Identify the readers
Knowing who will be reading your publication dictates your writing style and your presentation of the text. Since the company employees will read the Image Masters newsletter, it should be informative but retain a sense of humor. Marjorie knows that clients sometimes read the newsletter, so she'll make sure that they are mentioned and that the newsletter always portrays Image Masters positively.

Prominently feature the company logo
The Image Masters logo appears on all its print material: letterhead, envelopes, business cards, and advertisements. Naturally, Marjorie wants to include the logo in the newsletter. The logo reinforces the identity of the company.

Replace placeholders with text
The Catalog includes text frames as placeholders in its page design. These **placeholders** contain nonsense Latin text that can easily be replaced with typed text or previously created Word documents. This fake text lets you see how text looks on the page, without being distracted by its content. Marjorie can easily replace these placeholders with meaningful text.

Emphasize certain text
Some text on a page should stand out. Refer to Figure B-1. Marjorie will use a pull quote to pique the interest of readers. She'll use a sidebar to add emphasis to a particular article.

Pull quote text is taken from a story

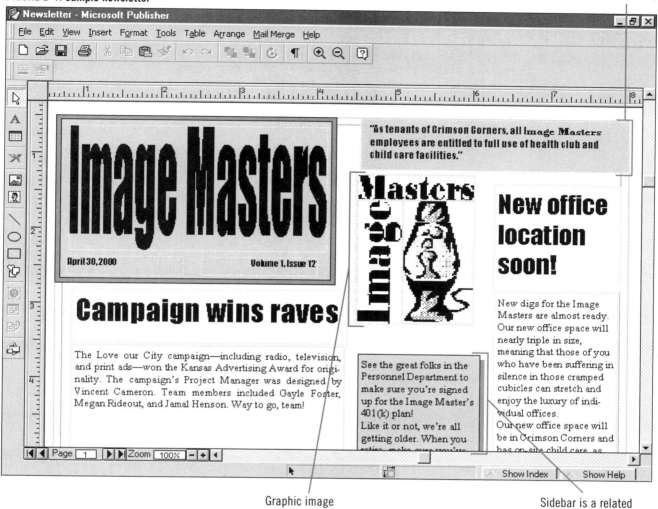

Graphic image

Sidebar is a related story with formatting to add emphasis

Publisher 98

Creating a Publication with the Catalog

The Catalog wizards make it easy to choose the type of publication you want. After answering a few simple questions, a wizard creates all the necessary elements you need to get started quickly. Marjorie uses the Catalog wizards to create a newsletter.

Steps

Trouble?

If Publisher is already open, to open the Catalog dialog box, click File on the menu bar, click New, then select a wizard. If you don't see wizards displayed in the Catalog dialog box, see your instructor or technical support person.

1. Start Publisher

The Catalog dialog box opens. This dialog box contains tabs that let you choose among Publications by Wizard, Publications by Design, Blank Publications, or Existing Publications. The default selection is the Newsletters Wizard, as shown in Figure B-2.

2. Click the Blocks Newsletter, then click Start Wizard

The Newsletter Wizard displays a series of dialog boxes in which you specify the features of your publication. In the first dialog box, you select a color scheme.

3. Click Next, then click Tropics

Compare your screen to Figure B-3. As you click each sample palette, the page sample changes.

4. Click Next

The next dialog boxes let you choose how many columns should appear on each page, whether a placeholder should be used for a customer address, how the newsletter should be printed, and what type of information will be included in the publication.

5. Click Next to accept the default value of three columns, click Next to accept the address placeholder default, then click Finish to accept double-sided printing

The newsletter displays in the workspace, as shown in Figure B-4. You decide to save your work for later use.

6. Click the Save button 🖫 on the Standard toolbar, locate your Project Disk by clicking the Save in list arrow, type Newsletter 1 in the File name text box, then click Save

Types of Catalog publications

The Catalog is a visual directory containing more than 1600 different types of publications. Most of those choices are available in the Catalog dialog box. Each template offers a variety of choices within its particular category. Brochures, for example, are available in many different styles and layout schemes. Labels can be created for floppy disks, audio and video cassettes, and CD case liners.

FIGURE B-2: Catalog dialog box

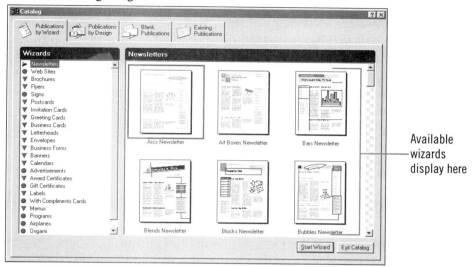

Available wizards display here

FIGURE B-3: First screen in Newsletter Wizard

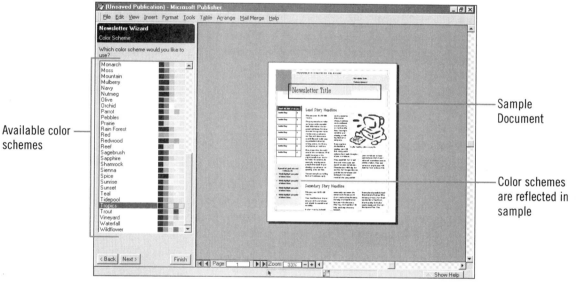

Available color schemes

Sample Document

Color schemes are reflected in sample

FIGURE B-4: Completed newsletter

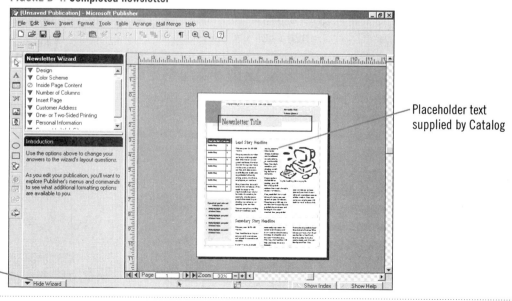

Placeholder text supplied by Catalog

Click to close Wizard Help window

Replacing Frame Text

Text can either be typed directly into a frame or you can insert documents created in a word processor, such as Microsoft Word. Since the Catalog created placeholders for you, you can utilize the existing text frames.  Marjorie needs to replace the placeholders in the newsletter she created earlier with the text she has written. She inserts a Word document and types replacement text.

Steps

1. Click the **Open button** 📂 on the Standard toolbar, open the file **Pub B-1** from your Project Disk, click **OK** to initialize the printer if necessary, click **Yes** to update embedded objects if necessary, then save the file as **IM Newsletter**

QuickTip

Turn off individual tippage displays by pressing [Esc].

2. Click the **Secondary Article Heading**, as shown in Figure B-5
   Handles surround the selected text. A balloon with help text may appear next to the selected text. This assistance is called a **tippage**. To turn tippages on or off, click Tools on the menu bar, click Options, click the Editing and User Assistance tab, click the Show tippages check box to deselect it, then click OK. Next, you decide to zoom into the selected text for a closer look.

QuickTip

You can zoom by clicking the Select Zoom Mode button, which always displays the Zoom factor, or click the Zoom In and Zoom Out buttons.

3. Press **[F9]**
   You may have to use the scroll bars to position the selected text. You type the new text for this heading.

4. Press **[Ctrl][A]** to select the text, then type **New Office Location Soon!**
   The typed text replaces the text placeholder. You select the column beneath the heading that contains nonsense Latin words, and delete the placeholder text prior to replacing it with text from a Word document.

5. Click the **column** below this heading, Press **[Ctrl][A]** to select the text, then press **[Delete]**
   Now that the text frame is empty, you insert an existing Word document into it.

QuickTip

Instead of using the menu bar, you can right-click the text frame, point to Change Text, then click Text File.

6. Click **Insert** on the menu bar, click **Text File**, locate the files on your Project Disk, click **PUB B-2**, then click **OK**
   You might have to use the scroll buttons to see the new text. Compare your newsletter to Figure B-6. You zoom out so the newsletter fills the screen and then save your work.

7. Press **[F9]**, then click the **Save button** 💾

FIGURE B-5: Selected text frame

Toolbar displays when a text frame is selected

Handles surround text frame

Tippage

Secondary Article Heading

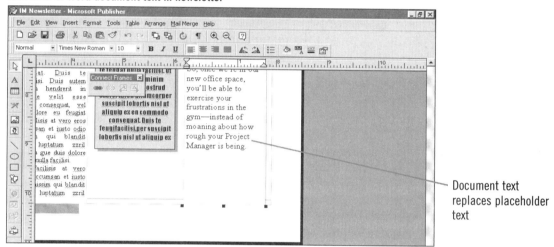

FIGURE B-6: Word document text in newsletter

Document text replaces placeholder text

Resizing a frame

A frame—whether it contains text or a graphic image—can be resized. Once a frame is selected, you can change its size by placing the mouse pointer over a handle and then dragging it. The pointer may change to 🔲, 🔳, 🔲, or 🔳, depending on the handle you place the pointer on. If, for example, the A••• button appears at the end of a selected frame, it may be possible to resize the frame, enabling the text to fit. Figure B-7 shows a text frame being diagonally resized to make it shorter and narrower.

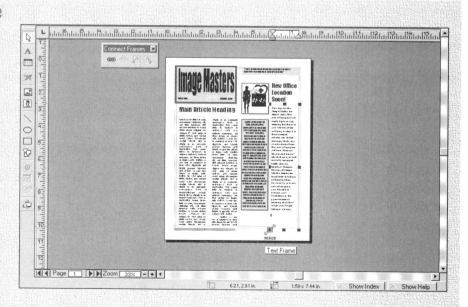

Publisher 98

Adding a Graphic Image

Artwork in a publication can express in feeling what might take hundreds of words to accomplish. In electronic form, a piece of artwork is called a **graphic image**. **Clip art** is a collection of graphic images supplied on a disk. Publisher comes with thousands of pieces of clip art, but artwork can also be scanned into your computer, purchased separately, or created using drawing programs. Table B-1 lists some of the common graphic image formats that can be used in Publisher. ✐ Marjorie incorporates the logo—already in electronic form—into her newsletter. She begins by selecting the graphic image placeholder and zooming to better view the image.

1. Click the **graphic image placeholder**, then press **[F9]**
   Handles surround the placeholder, indicating that it is selected. Next, you replace the placeholder artwork with the electronic logo file.

2. Click **Insert** on the menu bar, point to **Picture**, then click **From File**
   The Insert Picture File dialog box opens. You use the Im-logo file.

3. Click the **Look in list arrow**, locate your Project Disk, click **Im-logo** as shown in Figure B-8, then click **OK**
   Publisher realizes that the image being imported is a different size than the placeholder and opens the Import Picture dialog box, which offers you two choices. The Image Masters logo displays in place of the graphic placeholder. Images can be resized by placing the pointer over a handle and then dragging the frame edge to specify the new size. The object's size and position are reflected in the status bar as you drag the pointer using the ruler coordinates. To preserve an image's scale while increasing or decreasing its size, press and hold the [Shift] key while dragging the frame's edge. You want the image to be in the same location, but larger, while retaining the same scale.

> **QuickTip**
>
> Ruler coordinates in this book are given as follows: 1¼" V/6" H means 1¼" on the vertical ruler, 6" on the horizontal ruler.

4. Place the pointer over the upper-right handle of the image so it turns to ⬈ RESIZE, press and hold **[Shift]**, then drag the ⬈ RESIZE pointer to 1¼" V/6" H, as shown in Figure B-9
   As you drag the frame, lines move on the rulers to guide your actions and the outline of the image changes in size. You want to see the full-page image.

5. Press **[F9]**
   Pleased with how the image looks, you save your work.

6. Click the **Save button** 💾

FIGURE B-8: Insert Picture File dialog box

Available graphic images appear here

Preview of selected file

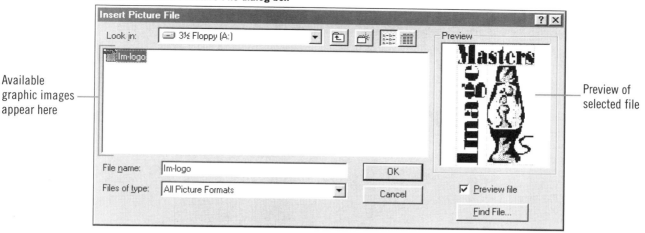

6" on the horizontal ruler

FIGURE B-9: Resizing a graphic image

1¼" on the vertical ruler

Outline of the image as it is being resized

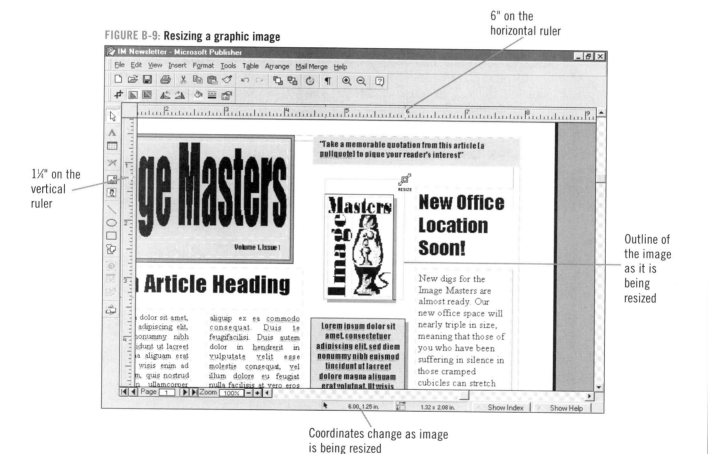

Coordinates change as image is being resized

TABLE B-1: Common graphic image formats

graphic image	extension	graphic image	extension
Bitmap	.BMP	Tagged Image Format	.TIF
PC Paintbrush	.PCX	JPEG Picture Format	.JPG or .JPEG
Graphics Interchange Format	.GIF	Windows Metafile	.WMF
Encapsulated PostScript	.EPS	CorelDraw	.CDR

Adding a Sidebar

Information not vital to a publication can make interesting reading when placed to the side of the regular text in a **sidebar**. A sidebar sometimes uses the same size font as regular body text, but it may also appear in a larger size or different font. Sidebars can be dramatized by adding a border or shading. ✎ Marjorie replaces the sidebar placeholder with text in a Word document. She starts by selecting the placeholder and enlarging her work area.

1. **Click the sidebar placeholder, as shown in Figure B-10, then press [F9]**
   Handles appear around the sidebar, which is enlarged to 100%.

2. **If necessary, use the scroll bars so you can see the beginning of the sidebar**
   While most of the body text in this newsletter is in the Times New Roman font, the Font button on the Formatting toolbar shows that the text in the sidebar placeholder is formatted in the Impact font. The Catalog created this style to make the sidebar stand out. By default, the sidebar text frame has a border, background fill, and shadow to make it stand out. Now you insert the sidebar text prepared in Word.

3. **Press [Ctrl][A] to select the text, click Insert on the menu bar, click Text File, click PUB B-3, then click OK**
   The new text displays in the text frame. Notice that the original formatting set up by the Catalog is still there. You want to see what the sidebar looks like without it. The shadow can be turned on and off using the Format menu.

4. **Click Format on the menu bar, click Shadow, then scroll as needed to view the top of the frame**
   Compare your work to Figure B-11. You decide you prefer the way the shadow looked, so you use the Undo button to restore the shadow.

5. **Click the Undo button [↶] on the Standard toolbar**
   It is a good idea to save your work early and often in the creation process, especially before making significant changes to the publication or before printing.

6. **Click the Save button [💾]**
   You want to see the full-page image.

7. **Press [F9]**
   All the text fits nicely inside the frame.

FIGURE B-10: Sidebar placeholder selected

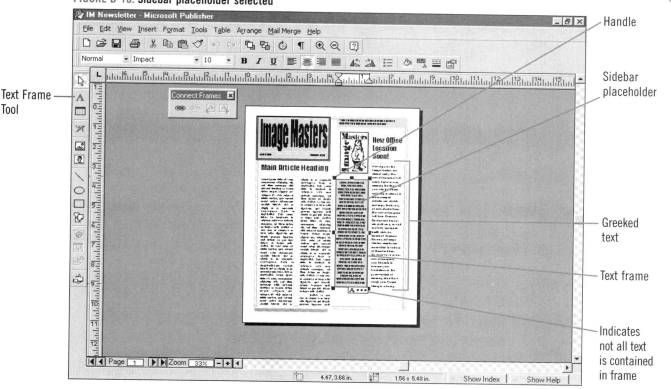

Text Frame Tool

Handle

Sidebar placeholder

Greeked text

Text frame

Indicates not all text is contained in frame

FIGURE B-11: Sidebar text inserted in publication

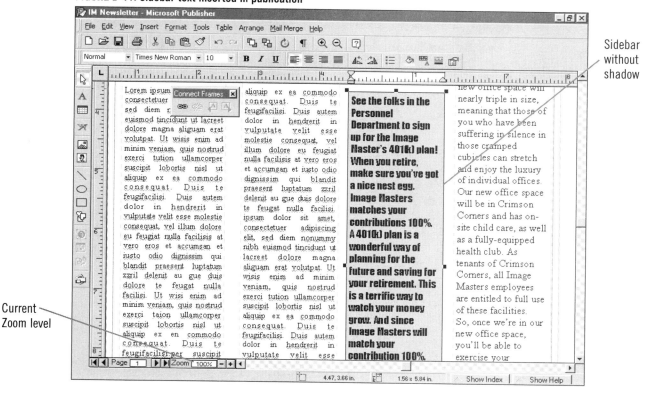

Sidebar without shadow

Current Zoom level

Adding a Pull Quote

To invite a reader to look at an article, a short statement or **pull quote** is often extracted from the text and set aside from the body of the text. Often the pull quote uses a different font and size from the body text. It does not have to be identical to text found in the body, but should be similar. A pull quote should be on the same page as the article from which it came, and in close proximity to it. It should also be long enough to be interesting, but short enough to be read quickly and easily. Marjorie puts a pull quote from the article on new office space at the top of the newsletter.

Steps

1. **Click the pull quote placeholder, as shown in Figure B-12, then press [F9]**
   The pull quote placeholder is selected and enlarged. Since the amount of text in the placeholder is small, you decide to type directly in the text frame. Newly typed text will automatically replace the selected placeholder text.

Trouble?
Depending on your computer system, you may be able to fit more words in the frame.

2. **Press [Ctrl][A] to select the text, type "As tenants of Crimson Corners, all Image Masters employees are entitled to full use of health club and, then press the space bar**
   The remaining words you have to type will not fit in the frame and you will not see them as you type. You will first complete the sentence, then adjust the frame size.

3. **Type child care facilities."**
   Only the first two lines of the typed text display, as shown in Figure B-13. You enlarge the text frame so the remaining line is visible.

4. **Place the pointer over the center bottom handle so it changes to ⬍RESIZE, then drag the frame edge to 1⅛" V**
   Compare your pull quote to Figure B-14. You want to see the full-page image.

5. **Press [F9]**
   Now you save your work.

6. **Click the Save button** 💾

FIGURE B-12: Pull quote selected

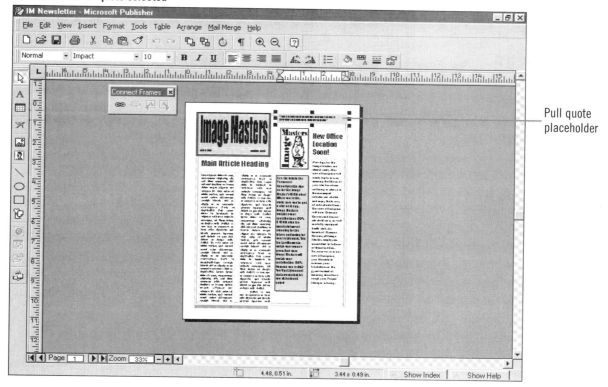

Pull quote placeholder

FIGURE B-13: Two lines of pull quote visible

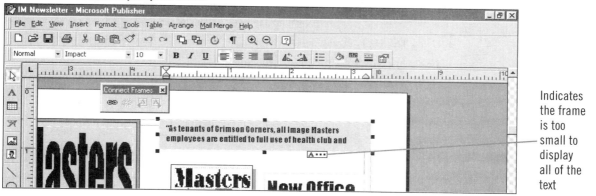

Indicates the frame is too small to display all of the text

FIGURE B-14: Entire pull quote visible

Drag frame to 1⅛" using vertical ruler

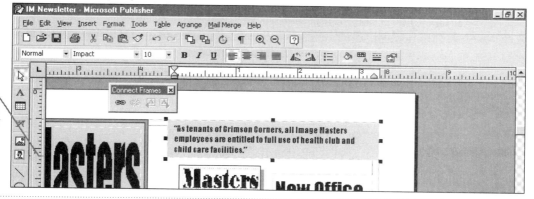

Using the Design Gallery

Publisher uses the Design Gallery to assemble a publication quickly. It also uses Design Gallery from within a publication to create an ad, calendar, coupon, or logo easily. The Design Gallery button—located on the Objects toolbar to the left of the workspace—guides you in creating these features. ✏️ Marjorie uses the Design Gallery to create an advertisement in the bottom-left corner of the newsletter. First, she deletes the two-column placeholder for the main article and replaces it with a new text frame and a single-column Word document.

Steps 1 2 3 4

1. Click the **left column** under the Main Article Heading, press and hold **[Shift]**, click the **right column** under the Main Article Heading, release **[Shift]**, right-click, then click **Delete Object**

   Both columns in the Main Article text frame are deleted. You insert a new text frame under the heading.

2. Click the **Text Frame Tool** 🅰 on the Objects toolbar, then drag the **+** pointer from ¾" H/3½" V to 4¼" H/6¾" V

   Now you can insert the existing Word document into this new text frame.

   > **Trouble?**
   >
   > If the text file doesn't fit inside the frame, delete the frame, then repeat steps 2–3, making sure to follow the measurements exactly.

3. Right-click the **new text frame**, point to **Change Text**, click **Text File**, click **PUB B-4**, then click **OK**

   The document is inserted into the text frame. Next, you replace the Main Article Heading placeholder with a suitable title.

4. Click the **Main Article Heading**, press **[Ctrl][A]**, type **Campaign A Success**, then click the workspace to deselect the heading

   Beneath the main article, you insert an announcement advertising a company garage sale.

5. Click the **Design Gallery button** 📷 on the Objects toolbar, click **Advertisements**, click the **Equal Emphasis Advertisement box**, as shown in Figure B-15, then click **Insert Object**

   The Advertisement object is inserted on the page, but is not necessarily positioned correctly. You want the object beneath the Main Article Heading and zoom in to see it.

6. Place the pointer over the object and drag the 🚚 pointer so the top-left edge is at 7" V/1" H, then press **[F9]**

   The ad displays in 100% magnification, as shown in Figure B-16. Next, you replace the heading text.

7. Click **Advertisement Heading**, then type **Garage Sale**

   Although you don't have all information needed to complete the advertisement, you enter the remaining information that you do have.

8. Click the text beneath the heading, type **July 25, 2000**, select the **Organization Name text**, then type **Image Masters**

   Your screen should look like Figure B-17. Display the newsletter in full-screen view, click the workspace to deselect the ad, then save your work.

9. Press **[F9]** to zoom out, click the workspace, then click the **Save button**

FIGURE B-15: Advertisements in Design Gallery

Tabs organize
Catalog
subjects

Triangle indi-
cates active
category

Available
Advertisement
wizards

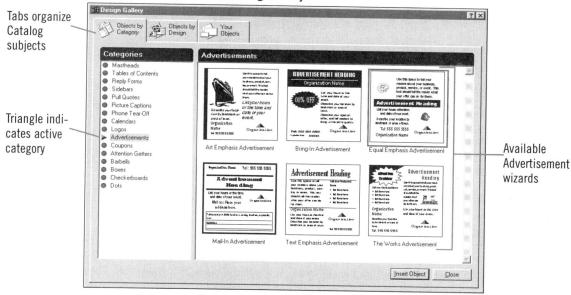

FIGURE B-16: Ad created by the Design Gallery

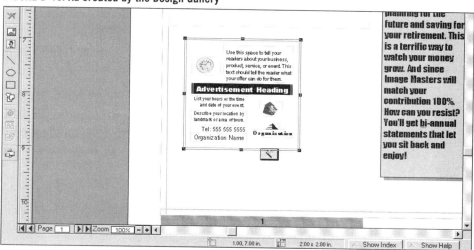

FIGURE B-17: Garage Sale ad

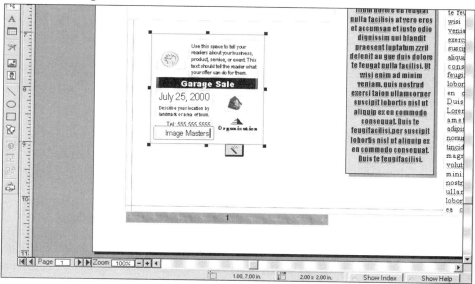

Grouping Objects

Once many objects are positioned on a page, you may find that you want to move one or more of them. Moving a single object is as simple as selecting it, then dragging it to a new location. But it gets more complicated when more than one object is involved. **Grouping**, or turning several objects into one object, is an easy way to move multiple items. Later, you can always **ungroup** them, turning the combined objects back into individual objects. Marjorie wants to reposition the Image Masters logo and the sidebar to better utilize the white space at the bottom of the page. Instead of moving the logo and story separately, she groups them and moves them as one object.

1. **Click the Image Masters logo, press and hold [Shift], then click the sidebar**
   Instead of black handles surrounding one object, gray handles surround each selected object, as shown in Figure B-18. You want to group the selected objects.

2. **Click the Group Objects button 🄶 🖬 beneath the selected objects**
   The two objects are now surrounded by a single set of handles, which indicates that the objects are grouped. The Group Objects button displays now as the Ungroup Objects button, as seen in Figure B-19. You reposition the grouped object.

3. **Position the pointer until the 🚚 pointer appears, then drag the top of the graphic image to 1¾" V**
   Since you grouped the objects only to make them easier to move, you ungroup them now that you are finished.

4. **Click the Ungroup Objects button 🄼 , then click the workspace to deselect them**
   Compare your newsletter to Figure B-20. You decide to save your work and print the newsletter.

5. **Click the Save button 🖫 , then click the Print button 🖨 on the Standard toolbar**
   A copy of the publication is printed. You end your Publisher session.

6. **Click File on the menu bar, then click Exit Publisher**

FIGURE B-18: **Preparing to group objects**

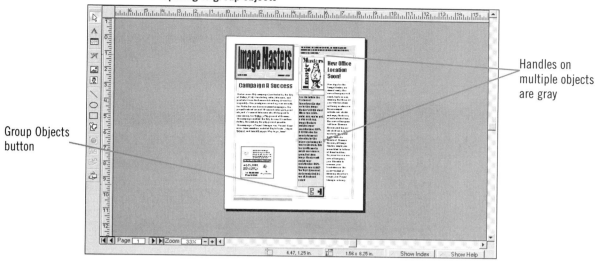

Group Objects button

Handles on multiple objects are gray

FIGURE B-19: **Grouped objects can be moved as a single object**

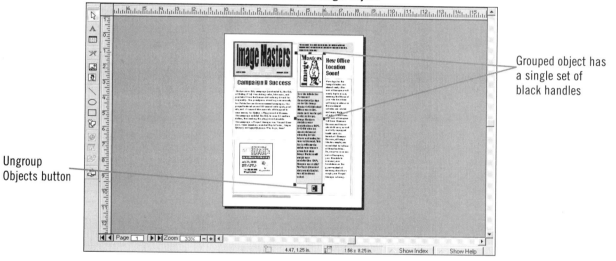

Ungroup Objects button

Grouped object has a single set of black handles

FIGURE B-20: **Completed newsletter**

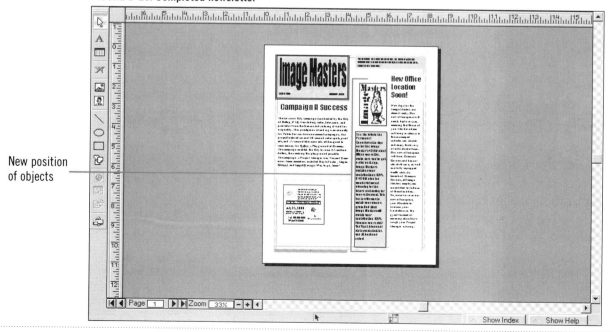

New position of objects

Practice

► Concepts Review

Label each of the elements of the Publisher window shown in Figure B-21.

FIGURE B-21

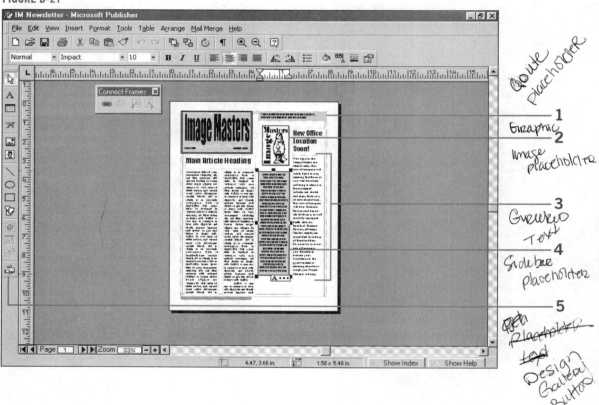

Handwritten labels:
1. Quote Placeholder
2. Graphic
Image Placeholder
3. Greeked Text
4. Sidebar Placeholder
5. Beta Placeholder text
Design Gallery Button

Match each of the terms or buttons with the statement that describes its function.

6. Creates an ad or logo E
7. Assistance that appears in a balloon D
8. Resizes a frame B
9. Creates a text frame A
10. Artwork stored in an electronic file F
11. Helps create a publication C

a. A
b. RESIZE
c. Catalog
d. Tippage
e.
f. Graphic image

Select the best answer from the list of choices.

12. Turn off an individual tippage by pressing:
    a. [Ctrl].
    b. [Alt].
    c. [Shift].
    d. [Esc].

13. Maintain scale while resizing a graphic image by pressing:
    a. [Esc].
    b. [Alt].
    c. [Shift].
    d. The right mouse button.

14. Which of the following extensions does not indicate a common graphic image format?
    a. .GIF
    b. .TIF
    c. .CDR
    d. .GFX

15. Interesting information that is not vital to a publication can be placed in a:
    a. Placeholder.
    b. Sidebar.
    c. Pull quote.
    d. Heading.

16. Which of the following statements about a pull quote is false?
    a. It should be on a different page from the actual text.
    b. It should be short and easy to read.
    c. It does not have to be identical to the text in the article.
    d. It should entice you to read the article.

17. Which of the following statements about graphic images is false?
    a. Scanned artwork can be used in Publisher.
    b. Artwork created in drawing programs can be used in Publisher.
    c. You can use only the artwork that comes with Publisher.
    d. You can use any electronic artwork in Publisher.

18. Which button is the Design Gallery button?
    a.
    b.
    c.
    d.

19. Which pointer is used to change the location of an object?

a. .

b. .

c. +.

d. ⬚.

20. Group objects by holding and pressing [Shift], clicking each object, then clicking:

a. ⬚.

b. Tools on the menu bar, then Group Objects.

c. ⬚.

d. Objects on the menu bar, then Group.

► Skills Review

1. Create a publication with the Catalog.
a. Start Publisher.
b. Using the Catalog, select the Newsletter publication type.
c. Select the Blends Newsletter, with the Trout color scheme, one column, and no customer address placeholder.
d. Use double-sided copying for a primary business.
e. Save this publication as Sample 2 Newsletter on your Project Disk.

2. Replace frame text.
a. Open the file Pub B-5 and save it as Brief IM Newsletter.
b. Select the Main Article Heading placeholder.
c. Replace the placeholder text with the following: "Office Space Scoop".
d. Select the main article frame, highlight the entire story, then delete it.
e. Insert the file PUB B-6.
f. View and read the article.
g. Save the publication.

3. Add a graphic image.
a. Select the graphic image placeholder.
b. Zoom in to view the graphic image.
c. Insert the picture file Im-logo from your Project Disk.
d. Change the frame to fit the picture.
e. Zoom out so you can see the entire publication.
f. Save the publication.

4. Add a sidebar.

a. Select the sidebar placeholder below the image.

b. Zoom in to view the sidebar.

c. Delete the placeholder text.

d. Insert the Word file PUB B-7.

e. View and read the sidebar.

f. Zoom out so you can see the entire publication.

g. Save the publication.

5. Add a pull quote.

a. Click the pull quote placeholder to the right of the newsletter main title.

b. Zoom in to view the pull quote.

c. Replace the existing placeholder text with the following: "I can't tell you everything, or there won't be any surprises. I can say that there isn't a garish color in the place."

d. Pull the bottom handle of the frame to 1¼" V.

e. Zoom out so you can see the entire publication.

f. Save the publication.

6. Use the Design Gallery.

a. Click the Design Gallery button.

b. Create a coupon using the Tilted Box Coupon.

c. Reposition the coupon under the sidebar from 7½" V/6" H to 9½" V/7¾" H.

d. Resize the coupon, using [Shift] to preserve the image's scale.

e. Zoom in to view the coupon.

f. Select the ad and zoom in to view it. Replace "Free" with "Hurry".

g. Replace the organization name with "Crimson Corners".

h. Replace the text "Name of Item or Service" with "Health Club."

i. Zoom out so you can see the entire publication.

j. Save the publication.

7. Group objects.

a. Select both the graphic image and the sidebar.

b. Group the two selected objects.

c. Move the grouped object so the top of the graphic image is at 1¼" V.

d. Ungroup the objects.

e. Save your work.

f. Print the publication.

g. Exit Publisher.

▶ Independent Challenges

1. The Chamber of Commerce would like you to design a flyer for its upcoming fund-raiser. The organization is trying to raise money for its Playground of Dreams, a playground that community members will actually build. The funds will go toward materials, playground equipment, upkeep, and refreshments for volunteers.

To complete this independent challenge:

a. Start Publisher if necessary.
b. Create a flyer using the Catalog.
c. Use the Even Break Fund-raiser Flyer.
d. Make up the information necessary, such as the location of the fund-raiser, the address of the Chamber of Commerce, and the date and time of the event.
e. Add any additional text necessary to create an attractive flyer.
f. Save the publication on your Project Disk as Chamber flyer.
g. Print the publication.
h. Close the publication.

2. You've decided to create an Hours of Business sign for the front door of your company. Use the Catalog to create this sign. Replace the existing text with your own.

To complete this independent challenge:

a. Start Publisher if necessary.
b. Use the Catalog to create a sign for a business.
c. Choose the Business Hours sign.
d. Replace the text placeholders with the hours that your business is open. (You can make up any hours you choose.)
e. Save the publication as Business Hours sign.
f. Print the publication.
g. Close the publication.

3. While you were recently ill, a co-worker did you a favor and helped you complete a project. You've decided you want to thank your friend by taking her out to dinner at a fabulous restaurant.

To complete this independent challenge:

a. Start Publisher if necessary.

b. Use the Catalog to create a Greeting Card using the Sun Thank You Card.

c. Use the ArtBit layout with a quarter-page top fold and any color scheme you choose.

d. Add a text frame to the first page of the card that expresses your gratitude to your friend.

e. On page 3, replace the placeholder text with your invitation to dinner.

f. Save the publication as Thank You Card.

g. Print the publication.

h. Close the publication.

4. Create a Web page for your community using the Catalog. This site should discuss features that make your community a great place to live or visit.

To complete this independent challenge:

a. Log on to the Internet and use your browser to go to http://www.course.com. From there, click Student Online Companions, click the link for this textbook, then click the Publisher link for Unit B.

b. You can type in your zip code and follow the links to other Web sites in your community. Take notes and save any information that you find relevant and want to include in your Web site design.

c. Start Publisher if necessary.

d. Use the Catalog to create a Web site for your community.

e. The Web page should consist of one page, using the style and background of your choice.

f. Use the name of your own community: you may use a postal or street address if you wish. Adding a telephone number, fax number, or e-mail address is optional.

g. Replace the text placeholders with your own imaginative text based on the research you did on the Web.

h. Save your publication as *<name of your community>* Community Web Page on your Project Disk.

i. Print your publication.

j. Close the publication.

▶ Visual Workshop

Use the Catalog to create a postcard for Image Masters that announces its new location. Use the Side Stripes We've Moved layout, the crocus color scheme, and show only the address on the other side of the card. Print one postcard in the center of the page for your primary business. Add the Im-Logo graphic image and replace the placeholder text using Figure B-22 as a guide. Save the publication as IM Postcard on your Project Disk.

FIGURE B-22

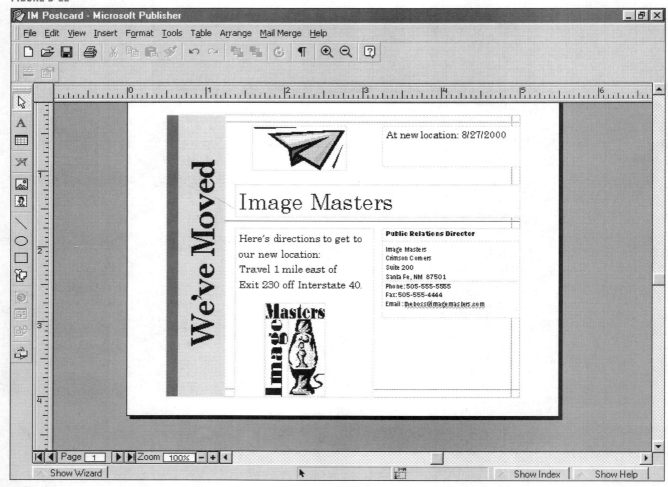

Unit
C

Formatting
Text

Objectives

- ► **Use layout guides**
- ► **Use ruler guides**
- ► **Work with a frame**
- ► **Add bullets and numbering**
- ► **Check spelling**
- ► **Use Design Gallery elements**
- ► **Paint formats**
- ► **Add a table**

You've learned the basics about creating a publication: using the Catalog, adding a graphic image, and replacing placeholders with text. Now you'll learn how to use more of the powerful tools available in Publisher. These tools help you design and lay out text and graphics to create publications that look consistent and professional. Jennifer Stockoff is the editorial assistant for Vintage Homes, a real estate company and Image Masters client. She is designing a newsletter that will be distributed to the realtor's clients. Jennifer uses many Publisher tools to create the newsletter.

Using Layout Guides

If correctly laid out, each issue of a newsletter publication has specific elements placed to achieve a consistent look. This consistency occurs only with careful planning. **Layout guides**, horizontal and vertical lines visible only on the screen, help you accurately position objects within a page and across pages in a publication. An unlimited number of blue and pink layout guides can be added to a page by pulling them from the vertical or horizontal ruler. ✎ Jennifer's first assignment is to lay out a four-page newsletter. She has already created the design and will set up the layout guides.

Steps 1234

QuickTip

To find out more information, type layout guides in the Help Index, then click View a demo on layout guides.

1. **Start Publisher, click the Existing Publications tab in the Catalog dialog box, click More Files, open the file PUB C-1 from your Project Disk, click OK to initialize your printer if necessary, click Yes to update embedded objects if necessary, then save the file as Vintage Homes Newsletter**
   Layout guides help you align elements on a page and exist on the background of each page. You want to modify the existing layout. You can easily add layout guides using the Arrange menu.

Trouble?

If the Layout Guides command overview step-by-step dialog box opens, click Continue.

2. **Click Arrange on the menu bar, then click Layout Guides**
   The Layout Guides dialog box opens, as shown in Figure C-1. You plan to add photographs of available real estate properties to your newsletter, so you create a grid that will have three columns and three rows on pages 2 and 3. These layout guides will be used to line up the photographs easily. Since this newsletter may be stapled, you accept the default **mirrored guides**, so that right and left facing pages will have opposite margins and layout guides.

3. **Click the Columns up arrow until 3 displays in the text box, click the Rows up arrow until 3 displays in the text box, as shown in Figure C-2, then click OK**
   The newsletter with the layout guides displays. The pink lines represent the column guides, while the blue lines represent the margins. Layout guides can be moved, but only when the publication background is in view. Switch to the background view and see how the design looks if the guides are moved.

Trouble?

If the Go to Background command step-by-step dialog box opens, click Continue.

4. **Click View on the menu bar, click Go to Background, then set Zoom level to 33% if necessary**
   The page view changes to background. Since mirrored guides were created, you need to move guides on only one of the pages.

5. **Press [Shift], place the pointer on the right layout guide on the left-hand page so that it changes to ↔, drag the pink layout guide to the 5" mark on the horizontal ruler, as shown in Figure C-3, then release [Shift]**
   Notice that when you released the mouse button, the layout guide on the right-hand page also moved. You decide to keep the columns at equal width. You use the Undo button to return the layout guides to the way they were.

6. **Click the Undo button ↶ on the Standard toolbar**
   The layout guides return to their original placement. You decide to return to the foreground view.

7. **Click View on the menu bar, then click Go to Foreground**
   The page view changes to display the foreground of the first page. The layout guides are visible on each page of the publication. Pleased with the inserted layout guides, you save your work.

8. **Click the Save button 💾 on the Standard toolbar**

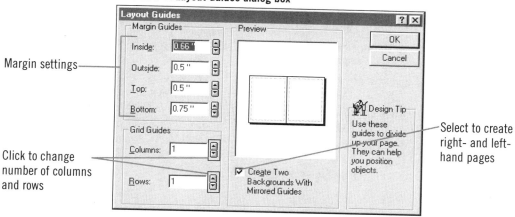

FIGURE C-1: Layout Guides dialog box

Margin settings

Click to change number of columns and rows

Select to create right- and left-hand pages

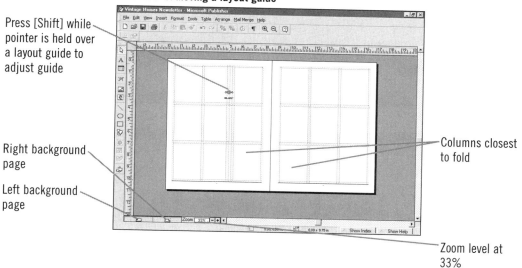

FIGURE C-2: Layout Guides dialog box with defined columns and rows

New column and row layout guides display here

New column and row settings

Facing pages will have opposite margins and layout guides

FIGURE C-3: Moving a layout guide

Press [Shift] while pointer is held over a layout guide to adjust guide

Right background page

Left background page

Columns closest to fold

Zoom level at 33%

Using different types of margins

When you think of margins, you probably think of the white space surrounding the four edges of a page. However, margins may be used to create white space anywhere on the page for clarity. Without them, the page would look cluttered and be hard to read. Margins occur around a graphic image, around each side of a column, and within a table or text frame. Any frame on a page has adjustable margins that can be changed by right-clicking the object, clicking Change Frame, then selecting the Text (or Object) Frame Properties—usually the next-to-the-last command in the pop-up menu.

Using Ruler Guides

In addition to the power of layout guides, Publisher also offers ruler guides. **Ruler guides** work just like layout guides but are created in the foreground of individual pages. (Layout guides are on the background of *each* page in a publication.) Visually, ruler guides are green horizontal and vertical lines that are dragged from the rulers into the workspace. The location of zero, the **zero point**, on both the vertical and horizontal rulers can be moved, giving you the flexibility to make precise measurements from any point you choose. ✎ Jennifer moves each ruler's zero point and adds ruler guides for the location of a graphic image on the first page. First, she moves the vertical ruler closer to the page.

Steps 1 2 3 4

Trouble?

If the Ruler Guide tip page displays, press [Esc].

1. **Click the vertical ruler, when the pointer changes to ↔, drag the vertical ruler to the left edge of the publication, as shown in Figure C-4**

   When you move a ruler, the zero point does not change, it just moves closer to the publication to make it easier to locate positions. You decide not to move the horizontal ruler since it is close enough to the top of the page. Currently, the horizontal and vertical zero point is set at the top-left edge of the page. Since you want to determine exact measurements from a particular location, you decide to move the horizontal and vertical zero point to the left edge and top margin. You can reset the zero point by double-clicking each ruler or by double-clicking the Move Both Rulers button at the intersection of both rulers.

Trouble?

If you can't find 5/8" on the horizontal ruler, press [F9] to zoom in, complete the step, then press [F9] to zoom out.

2. **Position the mouse over the Move Both Rulers button, press and hold [Shift] while right-clicking the Move Both Rulers button, drag the ↖ pointer to ½" V/⅝" H, release the mouse button, then release [Shift]**

   Compare your rulers and zero points to those shown in Figure C-5. Now you are ready to add ruler guides, sometimes called ruler guide lines. You want a graphic image to appear 4" from the left margin and 5" from the top margin. Create a vertical ruler guide.

QuickTip

Use the horizontal ruler to measure a vertical ruler guide; use the vertical ruler to measure a horizontal ruler guide.

3. **Press and hold [Shift], position the pointer anywhere over the vertical ruler, drag the ⇹ ADJUST pointer to the 4" mark on the horizontal ruler, then release [Shift]**

   A green vertical ruler guide appears on the page at the 4" horizontal mark. Now, you create the horizontal ruler guide. Use the same techniques to create a horizontal ruler guide, using the horizontal pointers.

4. **Press and hold [Shift], position the pointer over the horizontal ruler, drag the ⬍ ADJUST pointer to the 5" mark on the vertical ruler, then release [Shift]**

   After looking at the horizontal ruler guide, you realize its position is too low. You raise this ruler guide to the 4" mark on the vertical ruler.

5. **Press and hold [Shift], position the pointer over the horizontal ruler guide until it changes to ⬍ ADJUST, drag the ruler guide to 4" on the vertical ruler as shown in Figure C-6, then release [Shift]**

   The ruler guides appear only on this page and will be helpful when a text frame is added. Now you save your work.

6. **Click the Save button 🖫 on the Standard toolbar**

FIGURE C-4: **Moving a ruler**

Move Both Rulers button

New location of vertical ruler

Current zero point

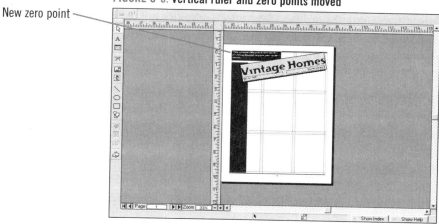

FIGURE C-5: **Vertical ruler and zero points moved**

New zero point

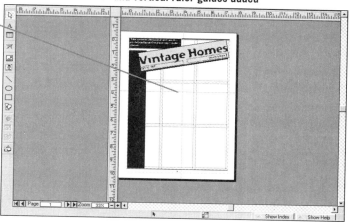

FIGURE C-6: **Horizontal and vertical ruler guides added**

Press and hold [Shift] while dragging a ruler guide

CLUES TO USE

Using Snap To commands

Publisher's Snap To commands let you take advantage of the layout and ruler guides. Turning on Snap To commands—Snap to Ruler Marks, Snap to Guides, and Snap to Objects—gives these guides a magnet-like effect, pulling whatever you're trying to line up toward the guide. Each of the Snap To commands is located on the Tools menu. Once the Snap To command is turned on, select the frame or object, move the pointer over the object until it changes to 🚐, then drag the object's edge toward the new location until the object snaps to the guide.

Working with a Frame

Once a frame is added to a page, it can be moved or resized. A border can be added to enhance the appearance of the publication and to make an article stand out. This border can display in any color and line width you choose and can be applied simply by clicking a button on the Formatting toolbar. The **Formatting toolbar**, which is visible only when text is selected, contains buttons for the most common commands used for improving the appearance of text and graphics. Which buttons appear on the Formatting toolbar depends on the selected object. Jennifer wants to add a text frame placeholder that will contain helpful hints for clients. She will try placing the frame using the ruler guides, but she may have to resize it until it looks right. She creates a text frame with a thick red border and places it on the first page using the ruler guides.

Trouble?
If the Connect Frames toolbar is not showing, click Tools on the menu bar, then click Text Frame Connecting.

1. **Click the Text Frame Tool [A] on the Toolbox**
   The pointer changes to ╋. To create and place the frame, drag the ╋ pointer using the ruler guides.

2. **Drag the ╋ pointer from 4" V/2¼" H to 6½" V/4" H**
   Compare your page to Figure C-7. You decide to enlarge the frame to see how it looks if it occupies two columns. First you move the vertical ruler out of the way.

3. **Click the vertical ruler, when the pointer changes to ↔, drag the vertical ruler to the left edge of the workspace**

4. **Place the pointer over the left middle handle on the text frame, then drag the ▭ pointer to align the left edge of the text frame with the right edge of the black box**
   You like the wider text frame, and now want to give the frame a thick red border.

QuickTip
A frame must be selected in order to change its border.

5. **Click the Line/Border Style button ▦ on the Formatting toolbar, then click More Styles**
   If you wanted to create a black border, you could select one of the choices in the Border button's pull-down palette. Since you want to change the color and thickness of the border, you clicked More Styles to open the Border Style dialog box, as shown in Figure C-8. You could also change a border by clicking Format on the menu bar, then clicking Line/Border Style.

QuickTip
A color's name displays as a ScreenTip as your pointer passes over the color samples.

6. **Click the 4 pt line border thickness, click the Color list arrow, click More Colors, click the Red color box, click OK to close the color palette, then click OK**
   The frame displays with the thicker, red border, as shown in Figure C-9. Satisfied with the changes in the frame, you save your work.

7. **Click the Save button ▦ on the Standard toolbar**

FIGURE C-7: Creating a text frame within ruler guides

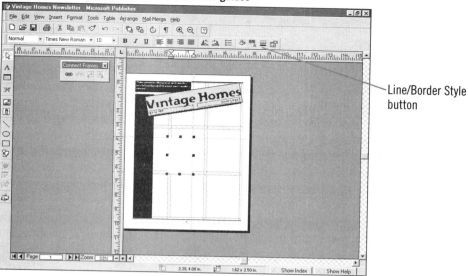

Line/Border Style button

FIGURE C-8: Border Style dialog box

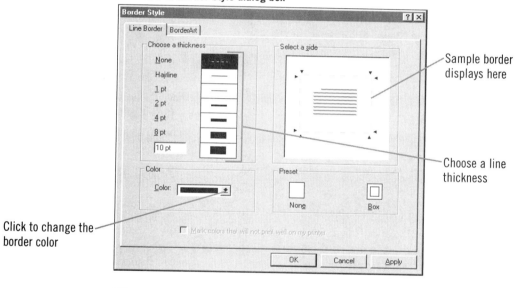

Sample border displays here

Choose a line thickness

Click to change the border color

FIGURE C-9: Frame with red, thick border

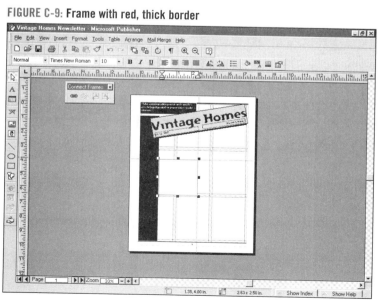

Adding Bullets and Numbering

Using paragraphs works well when you are telling a story. When you need to display information within a document in list form, you can add emphasis to the list by formatting the items with bullets or numbers. A numbered list is generally used to present items that occur in a particular sequence, while items in a bulleted list can occur in any order. Numbers or bullets can be created while typing the text or by selecting existing text and clicking the Bullet button on the Formatting toolbar. You can also switch back and forth between numbers and bullets, trying different styles of numbers and bullets until you arrive at the right format. ◢ Jennifer enlarges the view of the area containing the new text frame, then types a sample numbered list in the text box she's just created.

Steps

1. Make sure the text frame with the red border is still selected, then press [F9]
   The text frame is enlarged. You type an introductory sentence in the text frame.

2. Type **Save yourself hassles and disappointments. Before looking at homes, prepare yourself by doing the following:**, then press [Enter]
   The numbered list will be typed next.

3. Type **Gather your state and federal income tax reports for the last three years.**, press [Enter], type **Pre-qualify with any bank or lender. (This should be free and carries no obligation.)**, press [Enter], type **Choose a realtor with whom you feel comfortable—this should be fun.**, press [Enter], type **Think carefully about what features you really want, and where you want to live.**, then press [Enter]
   Compare your text with Figure C-10. Before applying numbers or bullets, you first must select the text you want to format, then click the Bulleted or Numbered List button to apply the formatting.

4. Drag the I pointer to select the text from **Gather** to the word **live.** so that the last four sentences are selected, then click the **Bullets button** ☰ on the Formatting toolbar
   If you wanted to use one of the bullets displayed on the Bulleted List palette, you could click it. Since you want to use numbers, you need to click More Bullets.

5. Click **More Bullets**, click the **Numbered list option button**, as shown in Figure C-11, then click **OK**
   The text is formatted as four steps, numbered 1 to 4. A new step begins wherever you press [Enter] in the text. You decide that items 3 and 4 should be reversed. This change is not a problem since Publisher will automatically renumber moved text in the list.

6. Click to deselect the text, drag the I pointer to select all the **text in item number 3** (*including the final hard return*), note that the pointer changes to ⬚DRAG, then drag the **selection** beneath item 4
   Compare your work with Figure C-12. You zoom out to see the full page.

7. Click [F9]
   Save your work.

8. Click the **Save button** 🖫 on the Standard toolbar

FIGURE C-10: Text typed for the numbered list

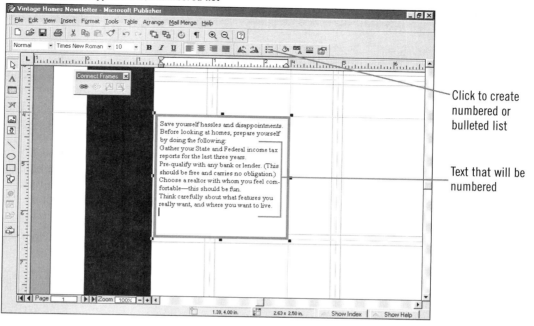

Click to create
numbered or
bulleted list

Text that will be
numbered

FIGURE C-11: Indents and Lists dialog box

Choose the type of
list

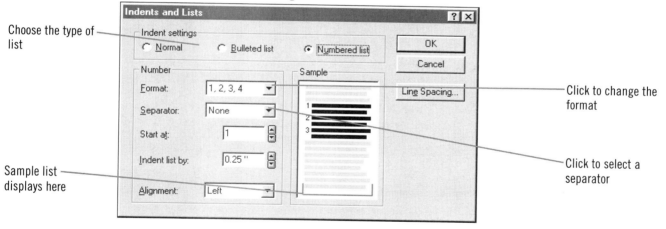

Sample list
displays here

Click to change the
format

Click to select a
separator

FIGURE C-12: Order changed in numbered list text

List is correctly
numbered

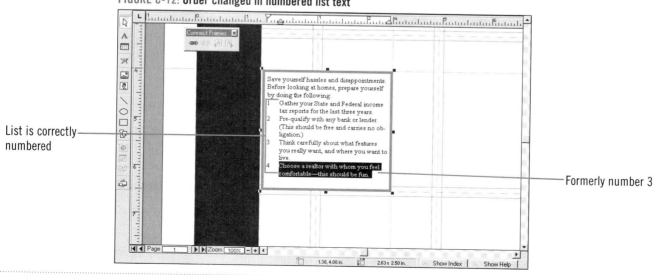

Formerly number 3

Checking Spelling

The most beautifully designed and written publication can be ruined by spelling errors. Fortunately, using Publisher's spelling checker means you'll never have to be embarrassed by misspelled words. You can easily check spelling by clicking the Spelling button on the Standard toolbar. Spelling errors are shown as you type, indicated by a wavy red underline. Correctly spelled personal or industry-specific words not already in the Publisher dictionary can be added. ✐ Jennifer imported text into a text frame on the last page of the publication. She checks the spelling for any errors.

Steps

1. **Click the Last Page button ▶ on the horizontal scroll bar, click the text frame surrounded by the blue border, then press [F9]**
   The text frame displays on the screen as shown in Figure C-13. Text in a text frame is called a **story**. You want to check the spelling of the story in this text frame.

2. **Right-click the selected frame, point to Change Text, then click Highlight Entire Story**
   Once the text is selected, you can begin to check the spelling.

3. **Click Tools on the menu bar, point to Spelling, then click Check Spelling**
   The Check Spelling dialog box opens, as shown in Figure C-14. The first incorrect word found is "faimily". You replace the incorrect word with the word already in the Change to text box. Often, Publisher correctly guesses a word's spelling and places it in the Change to text box, so you don't have to click a suggestion.

4. **Click Change**
   The spelling checker advances to the next misspelled word, stopping at "stressfuly". This word is used incorrectly and should be "stressful".

5. **Click stressful in the Suggestions box, then click Change**
   Continue correcting all spelling errors.

6. **Correct btuying to buying, correct recommendation, correct about, when finished click No in the warning dialog box, shown in Figure C-15, then click OK**
   Compare your corrected text to Figure C-16.

7. **Click to deselect the text, then press [F9]**
   Now save your work.

8. **Click the Save button 🖫 on the Standard toolbar**

FIGURE C-13: Spelling errors in text

Misspelled words

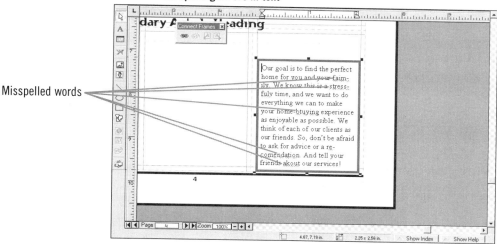

FIGURE C-14: Check Spelling dialog box

Click to change the misspelling to the selected suggestion

Choose not to accept Publisher's suggestion by clicking Ignore

Click to add the word to the dictionary

Suggestions for misspellings listed here

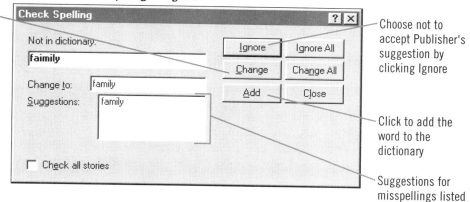

FIGURE C-15: Check Spelling warning box

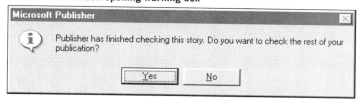

FIGURE C-16: Text after spelling is checked

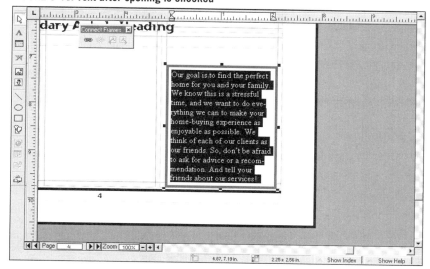

Using Design Gallery Elements

You can quickly add or modify elements using the **Design Gallery**, an assortment of designs for items such as pull quotes, sidebars, and titles. Each design in the gallery can be inserted or used to replace a selected object. Applying an existing element from the Design Gallery changes only the format: the content remains unchanged. This feature offers an easy way to change the look of a publication, without having to retype your work. It also helps to create a consistent style for elements in the publications. ➤ Jennifer wants to use the Design Gallery to change the look of the sidebar on the last page.

1. Click the sidebar located at 8" V/1" H on page 4, then press [F9]
   The sidebar placeholder is selected and enlarged. You delete the existing sidebar.

Trouble?

Be sure to click on a blank space in the sidebar, not on a misspelled word.

2. Right-click the existing Sidebar, when the pointer changes to 🚚, then click Delete Object

3. Click the Design Gallery Object button 📷 on the Objects toolbar
   The Objects by Category tab displays, as shown in Figure C-17. You want to reformat the existing sidebar with a design from the gallery. Formats from the Design Gallery can be applied to only one single ungrouped object at a time.

4. Click Sidebars, scroll down, click the Floating Oval Sidebar, then click Insert Object
   The design of the sidebar is changed to the Floating Oval design. Compare your sidebar to Figure C-18. You want to apply the same design to an adjacent pull quote.

QuickTip

The Design Gallery contains related styles for the various objects. This means that the Floating Oval sidebar can naturally accompany the Floating Oval headline.

5. Click 📷, click Pull Quotes, scroll down and click the Floating Oval Pull Quote, then click Insert Object
   Now you move and resize the object.

6. Move and resize the Pull Quote so it occupies the space from 5½" V/0" H to 6¼" V/3" H
   You zoom out to see the full page.

7. Press [F9]
   Now you save your work.

8. Click the Save button 💾 on the Standard toolbar

FIGURE C-17: **Design Gallery dialog box**

Types of designs
appear here

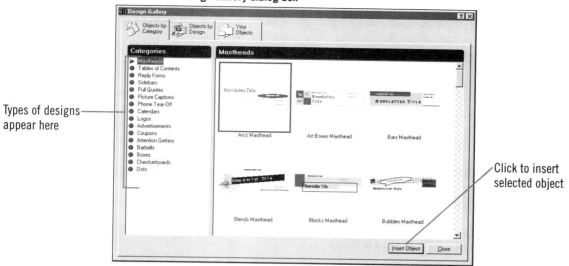

Click to insert
selected object

FIGURE C-18: **Floating Oval format applied to sidebar**

Design Gallery
Object button

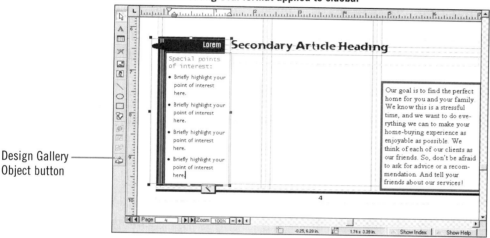

Using a Design Set

The Design Gallery contains many **Design Sets**—elements in the gallery that share common themes, colors, or objects. Figure C-19 shows the Southwest design set. You can also create your own design set by selecting an object, clicking the Your Objects tab, clicking the Options button, then clicking Add Selection To Design Gallery. The Add Object dialog box opens, allowing you to name the object.

FIGURE C-19: **Objects by Design tab in the Design Gallery dialog box**

Name of design set
appears here

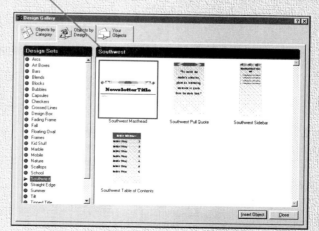

Painting Formats

Formatting buttons can be used to apply attributes such as bold, italics, small capitals, or different colors. To apply the attribute to existing text, select the characters, then click the appropriate button on the Formatting toolbar. This process can get repetitive, especially if more than one attribute is applied to characters. To help you apply formats easily and consistently, you can use the Format Painter button on the Formatting toolbar, or you can right-click the text and use the shortcut menu to pick up the formatting, and then apply the formatting. ▰▰▰ Once Jennifer applies formats to text, she uses the commands available to apply the same formatting to other text.

Steps 1 2 3 4

1. **Click anywhere within the text frame with the blue border on the fourth page, then press [F9]**
   The text surrounded by the blue border is enlarged. To draw attention to the first words in each sentence, you want to apply formats to the first two words. Begin by formatting the first two words in the first paragraph using buttons in the Formatting toolbar.

2. **Drag the I pointer over Our goal in the first paragraph, click the Bold button [B] on the Formatting toolbar, click the Font Color button [⊞A], click More Colors, click the Pink color box, then click OK**
   You also want this text to be underlined and in small capital letters. Both attributes are applied.

3. **Click Format on the menu bar, click Font, then click the Small caps check box**
   Compare your Font dialog box to Figure C-20.

QuickTip

You can also use the Character dialog box to apply formatting attributes found on the Formatting toolbar.

4. **Click the Underline list arrow, click Single, then click OK**
   Now that the formatting attributes have been applied, you are ready to paint them to other text.

5. **Click the Format Painter button [⊘] on the Standard toolbar, note that the pointer changes to ⬟?, place the pointer in the text box, when it changes to ⬟I, drag the ⬟I pointer over We know**
   You can also pick up and apply formats using the Format menu.

QuickTip

Pick Up Formatting and Apply Formatting can also be done using the Format menu.

6. **Click Format on the menu bar, click Pick Up Formatting, then drag the I pointer to select We think**
   You use the Format menu to apply the formatting you just picked up.

7. **Click Format on the menu bar, as shown in Figure C-21, then click Apply Formatting**
   All the text does not fit within the frame, but you can make it fit using copyfitting.

8. **Right-click the text box, point to Change Text, point to Copyfit Text, then click Best Fit**
   Now all the text is visible. You save your work.

9. **Click the Save button [💾] on the Standard toolbar**

FIGURE C-20: Font dialog box

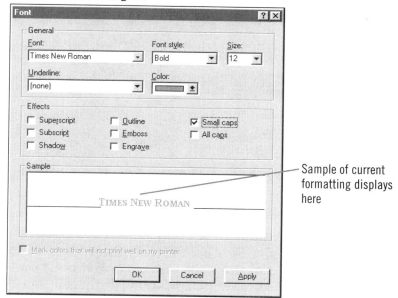

Sample of current formatting displays here

FIGURE C-21: Applying formatting using the Format menu

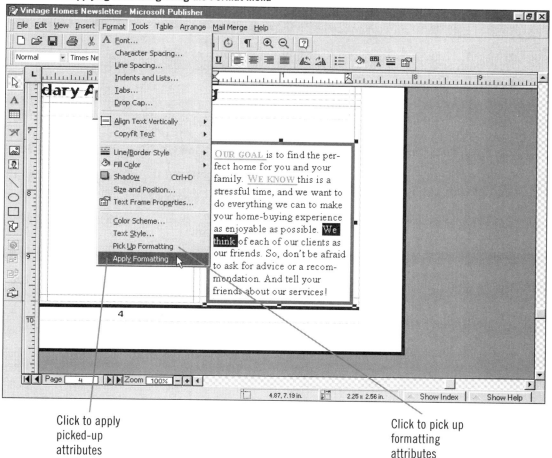

Click to apply picked-up attributes

Click to pick up formatting attributes

Publisher 98

Adding a Table

Some information is more easily understood if it is contained in a table. A table is created by first drawing a frame, then determining the number of columns and rows that are needed. Jennifer wants to include a table that contains several properties listed by Vintage Homes.

1. **Scroll to view the area between the blue border and the Floating Oval sidebar**
   The first step in creating a table is to draw a table frame.

Trouble?

If a Table step-by-step dialog box opens, click Continue.

2. **Click the Table Frame Tool 🔲 on the Objects toolbar, then drag the ╋ pointer from 7¼" V/1¾" H to 9¼" V/4½" H**
   The Create Table dialog box opens, as seen in Figure C-22. Publisher comes with 20 table formats that contain combinations of formatting, borders, and shading. Regardless of the table format you choose, you are free to change the numbers of columns and rows to fit your needs. You choose a table format and change the number of columns and rows.

3. **Click List 3 in the Table format list, double-click the Number of columns text box, type 4, then click OK**
   The table displays in the table frame. You can type directly in the cells of the table, pressing [Tab] to move from cell to cell. You begin by typing the column headings in the first row.

QuickTip

You can also navigate the cells in a table using the arrow keys.

4. **Type Address, press [Tab], type Bed, press [Tab], type Bath, press [Tab], type SqFt**
   When created, table cells are all the same width. Since the first column will hold the most information, you want to widen that column and make columns 2 through 4 narrower. When you place the pointer between column selector buttons, it changes to the Adjuster pointer. You change the width of a column by holding [Shift], then dragging the Adjuster to the new width. You move a column by placing the pointer on the column selector buttons and, when the pointer changes to the Mover, dragging the column to a new location.

QuickTip

Use the row selector buttons and press [Shift] to change row height.

5. **Place the pointer in the column heading between the Bath and SqFt columns until the pointer changes to ⟷ , press and hold [Shift], drag the ⟷ pointer to the 4" mark on the horizontal ruler, release the mouse button, then release [Shift]**
   You adjust the widths of the rest of the columns.

QuickTip

Clicking 🖨 sends to the printer all pages in a publication that have material on them. No blank pages are printed but borders on a page are considered material.

6. **Using the horizontal ruler as your guide, drag the ⟷ pointer to resize the Bed column to the 3⅝" mark, drag the ⟷ pointer to resize the Address column to the 3¼" mark**
   You are now ready to enter information in the table.

7. **Enter the table data using Figure C-23 as a guide**

8. **Click outside the table to deselect it, then press [F9] to zoom out**
   You are pleased with the way the newsletter is progressing and want to print pages 1 and 4 to see how it looks. You save, print, and exit Publisher.

9. **Click the Save button 💾 on the Standard toolbar, click the Print button 🖨 , then exit Publisher**

FIGURE C-22: **Create Table dialog box**

Sample of selected table

Available table formats

Recommended use

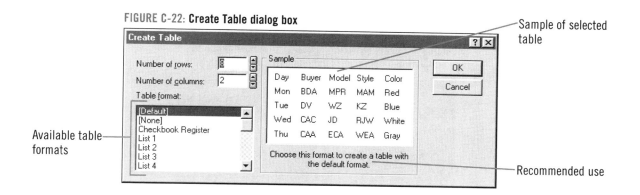

FIGURE C-23: **Completed table**

Column selector buttons

Row selector buttons

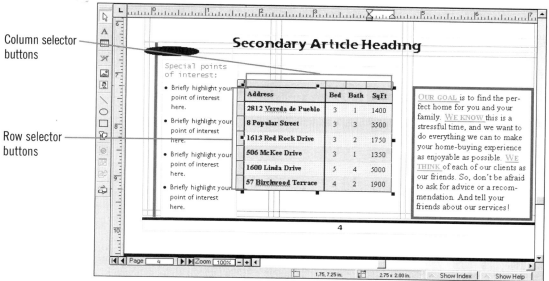

CLUES TO USE

Using AutoFormat

An existing table's design can be changed using the AutoFormat feature. The AutoFormat feature looks similar to the Create Table dialog box, except that it contains only table formats. Open the AutoFormat dialog box, shown in Figure C-24, by clicking Table on the menu bar, then clicking Table AutoFormat. Choose a Table Format, then click OK. Remember that you can change the number of columns and rows even after a table is created by using the Insert Rows Or Columns command on the Table menu or by right-clicking the mouse from within the table and selecting Change Table.

FIGURE C-24: **Auto Format dialog box**

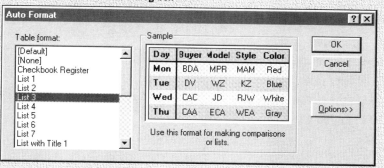

Practice

► Concepts Review

Label each of the elements of the Publisher window shown in Figure C-25.

FIGURE C-25

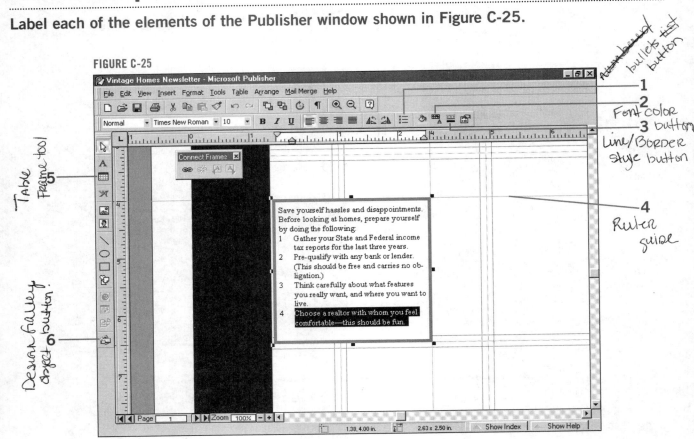

(Handwritten labels:)
- 1 — Attach...ed bullets list button
- 2 — Font color button
- 3 — Line/Border Style button
- 4 — Ruler guide
- 5 — Table/Frame tool
- 6 — Design Gallery object button

Match each of the buttons with the statement that describes its function.

7. Changes font color D
8. Opens the Design Gallery C
9. Paints formatting attributes E
10. Moves text B
11. Makes text bold F
12. Changes a column's width A

a. ⟷ ADJUST
b. ↖ DRAG
c. [icon]
d. [icon]
e. [icon]
f. **B**

Select the best answer from the list of choices.

13. Resize a column while holding:
  a. [Shift].
  b. [Alt].
  c. [Ctrl].
  d. [Esc].

14. Draw a table frame when the pointer turns to:
  a. ⬚.
  b. ▷.
  c. +.
  d. ⊹.

15. Ruler guides are:
  a. Blue.
  b. Green.
  c. Pink.
  d. Red.

16. Each of the following is true about layout guides, *except*:
  a. Objects can snap to them.
  b. They occur on every page in a publication.
  c. They appear in the background.
  d. They appear in the foreground.

17. Matching design elements can be inserted in a publication using the:
  a. AutoFormat.
  b. Design Gallery.
  c. Page Wizards.
  d. Design Checker.

18. Each of the following buttons is used for formatting, *except*:

  a. *I* .
  b. A .
  c. 🖌 .
  d. 🗛 .

19. Each of the following is true about tables, *except*:
  a. They can be formatted.
  b. The format cannot be modified.
  c. Column widths can be changed.
  d. Additional columns and rows can be added.

▶ Skills Review

If you complete all of the exercises in this unit, you may run out of space on your Project Disk. To make sure you have enough disk space, please copy files PUB C-2, PUB C-3, PUB C-4 onto a new disk, and files PUB C-5 and PUB C-6 onto another new disk. Use the new disks to complete the rest of the exercises in this unit.

1. **Use layout guides.**
   a. Start Publisher.
   b. Open the file PUB C-2 and save it on your Project Disk as House flyer.
   c. Add layout guides.
   d. Create two columns and one row within this publication.
   e. Save your work.

2. **Use ruler guides.**
   a. Move the vertical ruler closer to the page so that you can better view the workspace.
   b. Adjust the zero points of the horizontal and vertical rulers to the left of the vertical black bar.
   c. Create horizontal ruler guides at 2", 4", 5½", and 6¾".
   d. Create vertical ruler guides at 1", 2¾", 5¼", and 8½".
   e. Save your work.

3. **Work with a frame.**
   a. Add a text frame using the following dimensions: 2" V/5¼" H to 4" V/8½" H.
   b. Zoom in to view the text frame.
   c. Create a four pt violet border around the text frame.
   d. Zoom out so you can see the full page.
   e. Deselect the text frame.
   f. Save your work.

4. **Add bullets and numbering.**
   a. Select and zoom in to the text frame.
   b. Create a bulleted list using a diamond bullet that contains the information in Table C-1.
   c. Format the table text using a 14 pt Copperplate Gothic Light font.
   d. Zoom out so that you can see the full page.
   e. Save the publication.

TABLE C-1: Bulleted list information

Age of Home: 5 years
Square Feet: 5200
Bedrooms: 6
Baths: 4 full, 1 half
Levels: 3
Extras: gourmet kitchen, workout room, Spanish tile, more!

5. **Check spelling.**
   a. Select and zoom into the text frame beneath the bulleted list.
   b. Highlight the entire story in the text frame.
   c. Check the spelling of the selected text.
   d. You should find five spelling errors.
   e. Do not check the spelling in the rest of the publication.
   f. Zoom out so that you can see the entire publication.
   g. Deselect the highlighted text.
   h. Save the publication.

6. Use the Design Gallery.

   a. Click the Design Gallery button.

   b. Click the Attention Getters category.

   c. Click the Brick Attention Getter.

   d. Move and resize the object to 5½" V/1" H to 6½" V/2¾" H.

   e. Zoom in to the object.

   f. Zoom out once you've viewed it.

   g. Save the publication.

7. Paint formats.

   a. Select and zoom in to the bulleted list.

   b. Select the text Age of Home.

   c. Format this text using italics and Pink.

   d. Use the Format Painter to paint the Square Feet and Bedrooms text with the same formatting.

   e. Click the Format menu, then click Pick Up Formatting.

   f. Use the Format menu to apply the formatting to the following text: Baths, Levels, and Extras.

   g. Zoom out so that you can see the entire page.

   h. Save your work.

8. Add a table.

   a. Open the file PUB C-3 and save it on your Project Disk as Open House postcard.

   b. Create a table frame on page 2 from 2¼" V/3½" H to 4" V/7" H.

   c. Use the List 1 format.

   d. Create three columns and five rows.

   e. The column headings should be Address, Day, and Time.

   f. Enter the information in Table C-2.

   g. Resize the columns to fit the information, as necessary.

   h. Zoom out so that you can see the full page.

   i. Deselect the table.

   j. Save your work.

   k. Print the publication.

   l. Exit Publisher.

TABLE C-2: **Open House information**

Address	Day	Time
1414 Main Street	Saturday	1:00–4:00 PM
800 Beethoven Street	Saturday	9:00–11:00 AM
906 Leroy Street	Sunday	2:00–5:00 PM
33 Oak Street	Sunday	3:00–6:00 PM

▶ Independent Challenges

1. Your new client, the accounting firm called Count On Us, has hired you to design a postcard that tells its clients about its new office location.
  To complete this independent challenge:

  a. Start Publisher if necessary, open the file PUB C-4, and save it as Count On Us postcard on your Project Disk.
  b. Move the zero points to the top-left margin.
  c. Add ruler guides to the second page so you'll know where to include new information. Ruler guides should create an area for a graphic image, such as a logo, as well as an area for the new address.
  d. Insert a text frame and type the new address (which you can make up).
  e. Create a text frame in the area designated for the graphic image, then replace it with an element from the Design Gallery.
  f. Save the publication.
  g. Print the publication.

2. As the computer training coordinator in your company, you are often called upon to train new employees to use popular software programs. To mark the completion of your courses, you issue each student a certificate that describes the course he or she has completed.
  To complete this independent challenge:

  a. Start Publisher if necessary, use the Catalog to create an Award Certificate.
  b. Save the publication as Computer Training certificate.
  c. Move the zero points to the top-left margin.
  d. Create ruler guides for the insertion of each student's name.
  e. Create a text box for the student's name.
  f. Format the text frame border with a solid line, in any width and color you choose.
  g. Insert your name as the student completing the course.
  h. Use special formatting on your name.
  i. Save and print the publication.

3. Your brother-in-law has decided to offer delivery of lunches from his restaurant, Total Gourmet. He has asked you to create a menu that he can distribute to office buildings throughout the city.
  To complete this independent challenge:

  a. Start Publisher if necessary, open the file PUB C-5, and save it as Total Gourmet menu on your Project Disk.
  b. Create a table in the lower portion of the page that contains the menu. At a minimum, the table should include an item's name, brief description, and price.
  c. Choose the proper number of columns and rows.
  d. Select an appropriate table format and resize the columns as necessary.
  e. Enter items in the menu. (You make them up.)
  f. Save and print the publication.

4. You've been hired to create a Web page for a company called Relocation Services, a private company that specializes in relocating top-level executives. Although your client hasn't given you all the information you need, you have enough to create a skeleton layout.

To complete this independent challenge:

a. Log on to the Internet and use your browser to go to http://www.course.com. From there, click Student Online Companions, click the link for this textbook, then click the Publisher link for Unit C.

b. While connected to the Internet, search your favorite browser for companies offering similar services. Take note of the types of services they offer and the layout they use.

c. Open a one-page blank publication and save it on your Project Disk as Relocation Services Web page.

d. Create a heading with the client's name.

e. Add a text frame that contains a bulleted list of the client's services.

f. Format the text within the frame as necessary.

g. Add a colorful border to the frame.

h. Add an element from the Design Gallery to add emphasis to the page.

i. Save the publication.

j. Print the publication.

▶ Visual Workshop

Open the file PUB C-6 and save it on your Project Disk as Route 66 Film Society. Use Figure C-26 as a guide. Replace the descriptive paragraph with the heading shown; replace the paragraph beneath using the text shown in the figure. Save and print the flyer.

FIGURE C-26

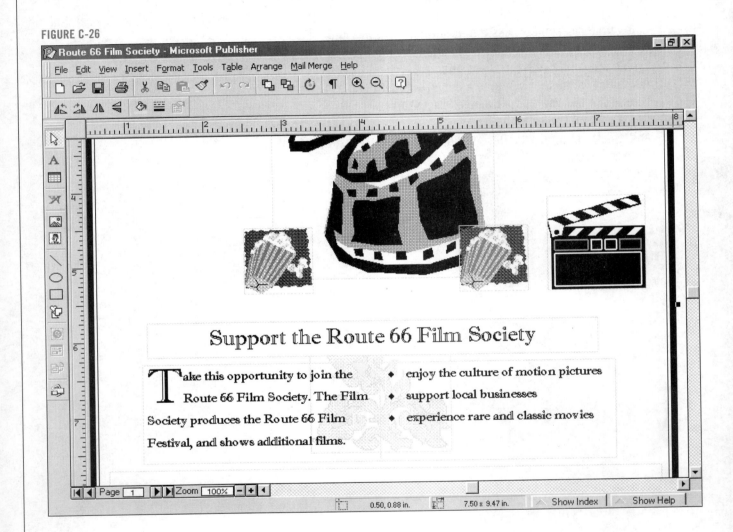

Working

with Art

Objectives

- ▶ **Insert and resize clip art**
- ▶ **Copy and move an object**
- ▶ **Crop an image**
- ▶ **Align and group images**
- ▶ **Layer objects**
- ▶ **Rotate art**
- ▶ **Use drawing tools**
- ▶ **Fill drawn shapes**

Publications should be attractive and easy to read. They are not—like novels—lengthy documents that require a lot of time to get through. Artwork enhances the understanding of a publication by complementing its text. Proper positioning of graphic images can relieve the monotony of text, add emphasis to the written word, and separate subjects. ✎ Gary Jeffries is the account executive for The Boundless Café, a new Image Masters client that sells books and Internet services in addition to operating a small coffee shop. His task is to design a promotional brochure.

Publisher 98

Inserting and Resizing Clip Art

Publisher's extensive clip art collection makes it easy to dress up any publication. There is so much clip art—contained in the **Clip Gallery**—that you can always find an image to represent a topic or round out a theme. You can use the Find feature and **keywords** to locate specific artwork. The Clip Gallery contains clip art, pictures, videos, and sounds and is not limited to the artwork that comes with Publisher. You can personalize your installation—any electronic image can become a part of the Clip Gallery. Gary has completed the text and design portion of the brochure for The Boundless Café. Now, he searches the Clip Gallery for an appropriate image, then adds and resizes it.

Steps 1234

QuickTip

The Microsoft Publisher 98 Companion (the manual that comes with Publisher) lists the contents of the Clip Gallery in its Pictures Gallery.

1. Start Publisher, open the file **PUB D-1**, click **OK** to initialize your printer, click **Yes** to update embedded objects if necessary, then save it as **Boundless Cafe brochure**
You want to enhance the brochure with art. To correctly position the image, you use the ruler guides to help you draw a picture frame on the page.

2. Click the **Clip Gallery tool** 🖼 on the Objects toolbar, then drag the ✛ pointer from 6¾" V/8¾" H to 7¼" V/9⅜" H
The Microsoft Clip Gallery 4.0 dialog box opens. The Clip Gallery contains sections that organize Clip Art, Images, Sounds, and Motion Clips based on content. Click the appropriate tab to access each section. You want to find a picture of a cup of coffee for the front of the brochure.

Trouble?

If you get error messages saying that you Cannot Open Preview Files or that the requested image is not available, contact your instructor or technical support person.

3. Click the **Images tab**, then click **Find**
The Find Clips dialog box opens.

4. Type **coffee** in the Match these keywords text box, then click **Find Now**
Pictures relating to coffee are displayed, as shown in Figure D-1.

Trouble?

If you do not have the images used in this unit, choose similar ones from the Clip Gallery.

5. Right-click the **coffee cup image**, click **Clip Properties**, verify the filename as **PHO2752U** in the Clip Properties dialog box, click **OK**, then click **Insert**
The image appears in the publication. Because the image is small, you zoom in for a better view.

6. Press [F9], place the pointer over the top-left corner frame handle until the pointer changes to 🔲ᴿᴱˢᴵᶻᴱ, press and hold [Shift], drag the 🔲ᴿᴱˢᴵᶻᴱ pointer to 6⅝" V/8½" H, release the mouse button, then release [Shift]
Compare the resized picture to Figure D-2. You are pleased with the resized picture. Zoom out and save your work.

7. Press [F9], then click the **Save button** 💾 on the Standard toolbar

FIGURE D-1: Microsoft Clip Gallery 4.0 dialog box after search

Categories in the Clip Gallery

Click to add selected image to publication

Click to start search

Pictures selected in the search. Yours may differ.

Image PH027526

Click to connect to the World Wide Web for additional clips

FIGURE D-2: Clip art picture inserted and resized

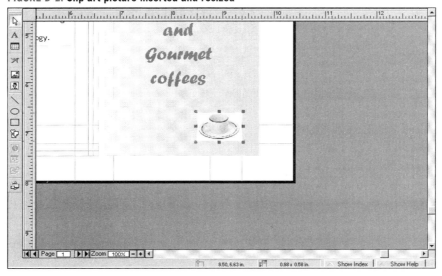

Browsing the Clip Gallery Live

Having access to the World Wide Web means you can easily add to the Clip Gallery using Microsoft Clip Gallery Live. This site offers a constantly changing selection of artwork. Figure D-3 shows the opening page of this Web site. This site lets you constantly update your clip art so you always have new, exciting types of artwork to include in your publications. You can download clip art, photographs, sounds, and video clips from this Web site.

FIGURE D-3: Microsoft Clip Gallery Live Web site

Copying and Moving an Object

Images can be inserted into a publication, then copied and moved to get just the right results. By copying artwork, you can create dramatic effects with duplicated images. A copied image is held temporarily in the Windows **Clipboard** where it remains until it is replaced with other contents or the computer is turned off. ✎ Gary has already inserted artwork on the page. Now, he wants to copy the image and move the copy to a new location. He begins by selecting the image and zooming in.

1. Click the image in the upper-left corner of page 1 of the publication, then press [F9] to zoom in
   An object can be copied using several methods. You copy the selected object by right-clicking it and selecting the command from the pop-up menu.

QuickTip

You can also copy a selected object by clicking the Copy button , then paste it by clicking the Paste button 📋.

2. Right-click the selected object, then click Copy
   Although it looks as though nothing has happened, the object has been copied to the Clipboard. Next, you paste a copy of the object into the publication.

3. Right-click the selected object, then click Paste
   A copy of the object appears overlapped on the original object, as shown in Figure D-4. The newly copied image is selected. You can now move the object within the publication.

QuickTip

Once it's on the Clipboard, you can repeatedly paste an object using whichever pasting method you prefer.

4. Position the pointer over the selected copy until it changes to 🚚, drag the selected object so the lower-right corner is at ⅝" V/2¾" H
   You can also copy a selected object quickly without copying to the Clipboard. To do this, place the pointer on the object, press and hold [Ctrl], drag the copy of the object using the quick copy pointer to the new location, then release [Ctrl]. If you release [Ctrl] before you release the mouse and place the object, you will move the original instead of copying the object. Use this method to create another copy of the selected image.

QuickTip

Holding [Shift] while you move an object moves it in a straight line.

5. Position the pointer over the selected object until it changes to 🚚, press and hold [Ctrl], press and hold [Shift], then drag the 🔍 pointer so the right edge of the copy is at 1¾" H, release the mouse button, release [Shift], then release [Ctrl]
   Compare your page to Figure D-5. The copy of the image is placed in a direct line to the right of the original object. You zoom out so you can see the full page, then save your work.

6. Press [F9], then click the Save button 💾 on the Standard toolbar

FIGURE D-4: Pasted object overlapping original object

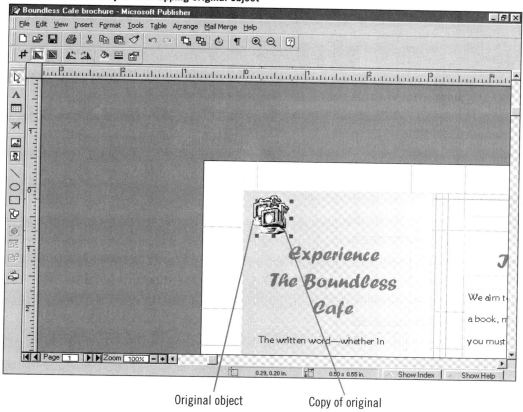

Original object   Copy of original

FIGURE D-5: Additional copies of artwork

Cropping an Image

Even though Publisher comes with thousands of images from which to choose, you may find that the art you've chosen needs some modification. Perhaps a picture's contents are not to your liking. In that case, you can always trim, or **crop**, portions of the artwork. A graphic image can be cropped vertically or horizontally—or both at the same time. Even though they are not visible, cropped portions of an image are still there—they are just concealed. ✎ Gary wants to crop portions of the sunset he has inserted on the second page.

Steps 1 2 3 4

1. **Click the Next Page button** ▶ **on the horizontal scroll bar**
   You want to zoom in on the artwork.

2. **Click the image in the center panel of the page, then press [F9]**
   Compare your page to Figure D-6. You want to crop the right side of the image so that the plant is concealed.

3. **Click the Crop Picture button** 🃏 **on the Formatting toolbar, then place the Cropping pointer** ⊹ **over the center-right handle**
   You drag the edge of the image so that the whole plant and all its components cannot be seen in the frame. The coordinates on the ruler are given as a guide: you should also look at the image as you trim it to be sure the correct parts are cropped.

   QuickTip

   To crop both edges simultaneously and equally, press and hold [Ctrl], then drag the ⊹ pointer.

4. **Drag the** ⊹ **pointer to 5" H**
   Next you crop the lower edge of the image. The Crop Picture button stays selected until you click it to turn it off, so you can continue cropping.

5. **Place the pointer over the center-bottom handle, drag the** ⊹ **pointer up to 2¼" V, then click** 🃏
   Now that the image is cropped, you want to resize it to scale.

6. **Position the pointer over the bottom-right handle so that it changes to** ⬔, **press and hold [Shift], then drag the** ⬔ **pointer to the ruler guide at 2¾" V**
   Next, you reposition the image. You want the image to appear centered in the column.

   QuickTip

   Don't worry if you see misspelled words; they will be corrected later.

7. **Position the pointer on the selected image so it changes to** 🚚, **then drag the selected image between 3⅞" H and 6" H**
   Compare your image to Figure D-7. Zoom out and save your work.

8. **Press [F9], then click the Save button** 💾 **on the Standard toolbar**

FIGURE D-6: Image before cropping

Crop Picture button

Crop these areas

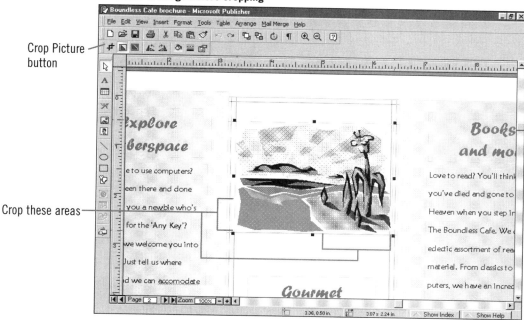

FIGURE D-7: Image cropped to scale and centered

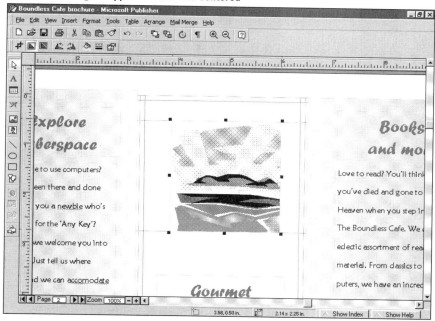

Recoloring an object

In addition to being cropped, images can be altered through recoloring. Once an object has been selected, right-click it, click Change Object, then click Recolor Object (or click Format on the menu bar, then Recolor Object). This method lets you change all the colors in the picture to different shades of a single color—ideal when creating a watermark effect. Figure D-8 shows the Recolor Object dialog box.

FIGURE D-8: Recolor Object dialog box

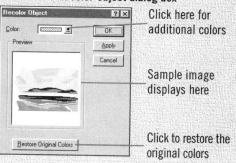

Click here for additional colors

Sample image displays here

Click to restore the original colors

Aligning and Grouping Images

Once you have inserted clip art, you can align multiple images so that the layout of the publication looks professionally designed. Artwork can be aligned from left to right or from top to bottom. Images can also be arranged in groups. A group makes it easy to move several pieces of art as one unit. ✐ Gary wants to make sure the three images on the first page are precisely lined up. Then he will move them as a group.

1. **Click the Previous Page button ◄ on the horizontal scroll bar, click the top-left image, then press [F9]**
   You want the bottom edges of these images to be lined up. You begin by selecting each of the images.

2. **Press and hold [Shift], click the second image, click the third image, then release [Shift]**
   All three images should be selected, as shown in Figure D-9. You use the pop-up menu to line up the objects.

QuickTip

You can also line up objects by selecting the objects, clicking Arrange on the menu bar, then clicking Align Objects.

3. **Right-click the objects, then click Align Objects**
   The Align Objects dialog box opens, as shown in Figure D-10. You want the objects lined up along their bottom edges.

4. **Click the Bottom edges option button, then click OK**
   Now that the images are all perfectly lined up, you want to move them down slightly on the page, closer to the text frame. First, you group the three images.

5. **Click the Group Objects button 🗗**
   The three selected objects are transformed into a single selected object. Now you can move the object to its new location.

QuickTip

You can move selected grouped or ungrouped objects by pressing an arrow key (on the keyboard) while pressing and holding [Alt].

6. **Drag the selected grouped object so that the lower edge of the frame is at ¾" V**
   Compare your work with Figure D-11. You ungroup the objects, then zoom out.

7. **Click the Ungroup Objects button 🔲, then press [F9]**
   Save your work.

8. **Click the Save button 🖫 on the Standard toolbar**

FIGURE D-9: **All three images selected**

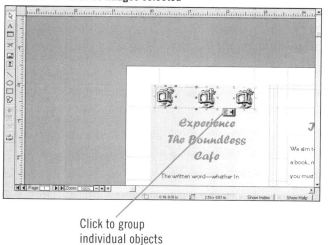

Click to group
individual objects

FIGURE D-10: **Align Objects dialog box**

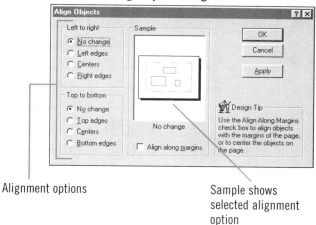

Alignment options

Sample shows
selected alignment
option

FIGURE D-11: **Lined-up and grouped objects**

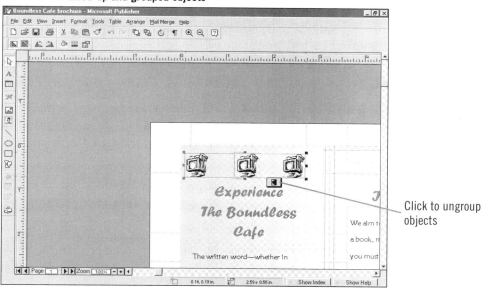

Click to ungroup
objects

Scanning artwork

If you have a favorite photo or piece of artwork that does not exist in electronic form, you can convert it to a digital computer file with a scanner. A variety of scanners are available in either a hand-held or flat-bed format. You can scan text, line art, or full-color images with amazing accuracy, enabling you to use virtually any image as clip art. Every scanner comes with its own easy-to-use imaging software. Publisher also lets you scan directly into a publication using the menu command shown in Figure D-12. (This menu command appears only if a scanner is installed on the computer.)

FIGURE D-12: **Preparing to scan an image**

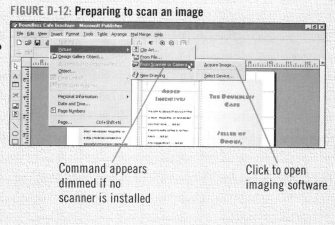

Command appears
dimmed if no
scanner is installed

Click to open
imaging software

Layering Objects

When positioning objects, you might want some images to appear in front of others. This layering effect can be used with any type of frame. You might want text to display on top of a shape, or you might want one image to overlap another image and a text frame to be in front of both images. You can send an image to the back (so it appears to be underneath an object), or bring it to the front (so it appears to be on top of an object). ◄▬▬▬ Gary wants to layer three objects on the second page.

Steps 1234

1. Click the Next Page button ▶ on the horizontal scroll bar, click the circular image in the lower-left corner, then press [F9]
   You want the image of the woman and disk to be at the bottom of the circle.

2. Select the image of the woman and disk, position the pointer on the selected image, when the pointer changes to ⊕🚚, then drag the image so its bottom-left edge is at 7" V/1⅜" H
   See Figure D-13. You want this image brought forward so that it looks like it's on top of the circular image.

3. Click the Bring to Front button ⬚ on the Standard toolbar
   The image of the woman and disk now looks like it is in front of the circle. Next, you want to move the image of the man and disk so that it is at the top of the circle and lined up with the image of the woman and disk.

4. Select the image of the man and disk, position the pointer on the selected image, when the pointer changes to ⊕🚚, then drag the image so the top-left edge is at 5½" V/1⅜" H
   The man and disk appear behind the circular arrow. You bring this image forward.

5. Click ⬚
   The man and disk appear in front of the arrow, as shown in Figure D-14.

6. Press [F9]
   Now save your work.

7. Click the Save button 🖫 on the Standard toolbar

FIGURE D-13: **Image before it is brought forward**

Click to bring an
object forward

Click to send an
object back

FIGURE D-14: **Both images brought forward**

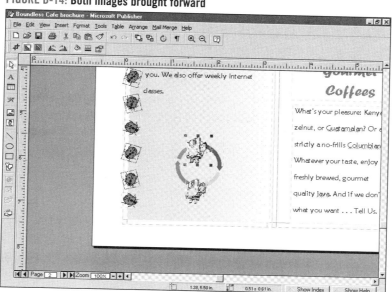

Layering text on an object

By creatively layering text and objects, you can make text appear on top of objects. Figure D-15 shows a text frame on top of many geometric shapes. By cleverly using the Bring to Front and Send to Back buttons, the text frame appears on top of all the shapes. Otherwise the shapes could easily obscure the text frame. The circles are in front of the turquoise burst, but behind the text frame.

FIGURE D-15: **Text box in front of geometric shapes**

Rotating Art

The **rotation** of an image—measured in degrees from a horizontal plane—can be changed using the Rotate pointer. You can rotate a selected object in 15-degree increments by pressing [Alt][Shift] or in specific degree increments by using the Rotate Objects dialog box. Artwork can be rotated vertically or horizontally by using the Rotate Right button or the Rotate Left button on the toolbar. Shapes created with Publisher's drawing tools can also be flipped; however, this feature is not available for clip art. ✦ Gary wants to rotate an object in the publication.

Steps

1. **Click the Previous Page button ◀ on the horizontal scroll bar, click the top-center object on the left side of the page, then press [F9]**
   The top-center image is selected and in full view on the screen. You want to see how the image looks rotated to the right.

Trouble?

If the Rotating Objects step-by-step dialog box opens, click Continue.

2. **Click the Rotate Right button 🔼 on the Formatting toolbar**
   The image rotates 90 degrees to the right. You decide to return the image to its original rotation.

3. **Click the Undo button ↺ on the Standard toolbar**
   Next, you decide to rotate the image a specific number of degrees.

QuickTip

Open the Custom Rotate dialog box by clicking the Custom Rotate button 🔄 on the Standard toolbar once an object is selected.

4. **Click Arrange on the menu bar, point to Rotate or Flip, then click Custom Rotate**
   The Custom Rotate dialog box opens, as shown in Figure D-16. You want to rotate the image 10 degrees.

5. **Click the Counterclockwise button twice, then click Close**
   The image is rotated 10 degrees counterclockwise. Next, you rotate the image in 15-degree increments using the Rotator pointer.

6. **Press and hold [Alt] and [Ctrl], position the pointer over the top-right handle so that it changes to 🔄 ROTATE, as shown in Figure D-17, drag the 🔄 ROTATE pointer to the right to rotate three increments to the right, release the mouse, then release [Alt] and [Ctrl]**
   Since the image is breaking up the text beneath it, you move the image up.

7. **Position the pointer over the selected image, then drag the 🚐 MOVE pointer to move the image so the top-left corner is at 0" V**
   Compare your image with Figure D-18. You decide to zoom out and save your changes.

8. **Press [F9], then click the Save button 💾 on the Standard toolbar**

FIGURE D-16: **Custom Rotate dialog box**

Each click rotates image 5 degrees counterclockwise

Enter a specific number of degrees

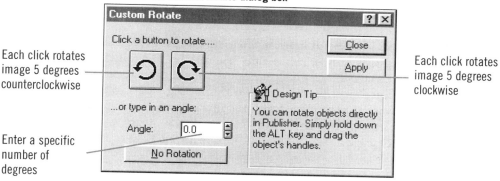

FIGURE D-17: **Rotating an object in 15-degree increments**

Outline shows new position

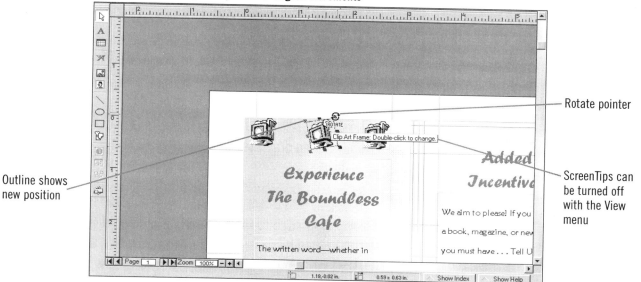

Rotate pointer

ScreenTips can be turned off with the View menu

FIGURE D-18: **Rotated image**

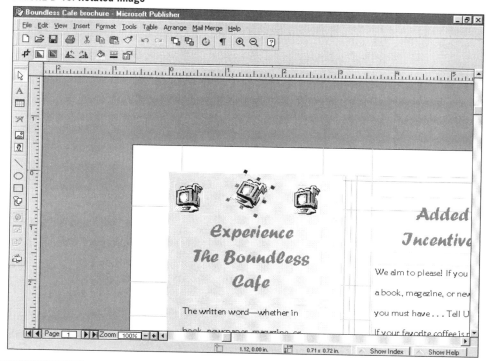

Using Drawing Tools

Publisher has a variety of drawing tools you can use to create your own geometric designs. The toolbox contains four drawing tools that let you draw lines, circles, rectangles, and custom shapes. Any shape drawn on a page can be moved, resized, or formatted to meet your personal design specifications. Shapes created with drawing tools can be flipped as well as rotated. This feature means you can create a **mirrored** image. A mirrored image has been flipped so that what was on the left side is now on the right side. Gary wants to fill an empty space with an original geometric design. He begins by drawing a border to frame the design.

Steps 1 2 3 4

1. Click the **Rectangle Tool** ▢ on the Objects toolbar
   You create the shapes by dragging the pointers to the size you need. You drag an outline for the box.

2. Drag the + pointer from 5¼" V/¼" H to 7¼" V/2¾" H, then press [F9]
   The box is drawn on the page and is enlarged. You want to add a thunderbolt to the design.

3. Click the **Custom Shapes button** 🔯 on the Objects toolbar, click the **thunderbolt** (on the far right side in the sixth row), then drag the + pointer from 5½" V/⅜" H to 7" V/⅞" H
   Compare your drawing to Figure D-19. You want to copy this shape and place it on the opposite edge of the box.

QuickTip

If you want to repeat a designed shape, create one with all the formatting attributes you want, then copy and paste it.

4. Press and hold [Ctrl], press and hold [Shift], position the pointer on the image, drag the pointer so the lower-right edge of the thunderbolt is at 7" V/2½" H, release the mouse button, release [Ctrl], then release [Shift]
   Now you flip this shape to create a mirror image.

5. Click the **Flip Horizontal button** ◣◢ on the Formatting toolbar
   You see how easy it is to create interesting and professional-looking design elements in a publication. You want to add one other custom shape to this design.

6. Click 🔯, click the **fifth burst** in the fourth row, then drag the + pointer from 5¾" V/1" H to 6⅝" V/2" H
   Compare your work to Figure D-20. Next, you save your work.

7. Click the **Save button** 💾 on the Standard toolbar

FIGURE D-19: **Drawing a custom shape**

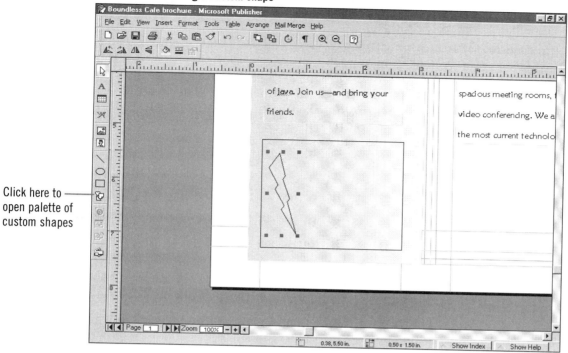

Click here to open palette of custom shapes

FIGURE D-20: **Design created with drawing tools**

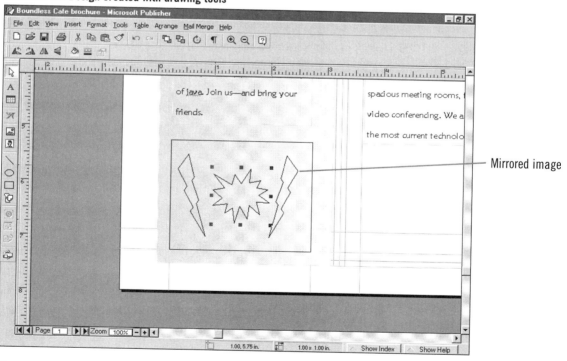

Mirrored image

Drawing perfect shapes and lines

Sometimes you want to draw an exact shape or line. To draw a square, click the Rectangle Tool ▢, then press and hold [Shift] as you drag the ＋ pointer. Press and hold [Shift] to create a circle using the Oval Tool ◯. Press and hold [Shift] to create a horizontal, vertical, or 45-degree angle straight line using the Line Tool ◥. To center an object at a specific location, click the tool to create the object, place the pointer where you want the center of the object to be, then hold [Ctrl] as you drag the mouse. Remember to always release the mouse button before you release the [Ctrl] or [Shift] key.

Filling Drawn Shapes

Drawn shapes can be left with their default attributes—displaying whatever background exists—or you can fill them using a variety of colors and patterns. Colors and patterns enhance designs and help you create elegant original graphics in your publication. Dialog boxes for colors and patterns can be accessed from the menu bar or by using a button on the Formatting toolbar. Gary would like to add color and patterns to the shapes in his design. He begins by adding color to the center burst.

Steps 1 2 3 4

1. Make sure the burst is selected, then click the Fill Color button 🖎 on the Formatting toolbar
   The color palette opens. ScreenTips will give you the color name as you drag the mouse over each color box.

2. Click More Colors, click the Medium Blue color box (second row on the left), then click OK
   The burst becomes blue. You want to add color and patterns to the left thunderbolt.

3. Click the left thunderbolt, click Format on the menu bar, point to Fill Color, then click More Colors
   The Colors dialog box opens, as shown in Figure D-21.

4. Click the fifth color box in the Red row [RGB (204, 0, 51)], then click OK
   Next, you add a pattern to the object.

5. Click Format on the menu bar, point to Fill Color, then click Fill Effects
   The Fill Effects dialog box opens, as shown in Figure D-22. The Sample box in the Fill Effects dialog box always displays the name of the selected style.

6. Click the 90% Shade pattern box to the right of the current selection, then click OK
   Now you pick up the formatting so it can be applied to the other thunderbolt.

7. Click Format on the menu bar, then click Pick Up Formatting
   The formatting can be applied to the other object.

8. Click the mirrored image, click Format on the menu bar, then click Apply Formatting
   Compare your work to Figure D-23. Zoom out to see the entire publication. You realize that misspelled words in any publication will reflect poorly on the client, so you decide to run the spelling checker before you save and print the publication. Then you exit Publisher.

9. Press [F9], click any text box, press [F7], correct all spelling errors, ignore all correctly spelled proper nouns, when you are finished checking spelling click the Save button 🖫 on the Standard toolbar, click the Print button 🖨 on the Standard toolbar, then exit Publisher

Trouble?

Unless you have excellent map skills, when working with one object among many, it's a better idea to use the menu bar to select a formatting command. If you right-click an object and select Fill Color, you might end up accidentally formatting the wrong object or even the page background.

FIGURE D-21: **Colors dialog box**

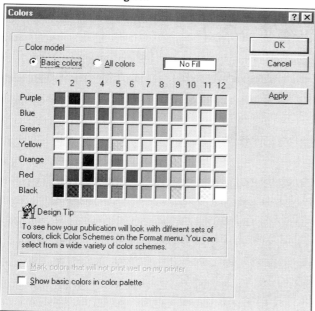

FIGURE D-22: **Fill Effects dialog box**

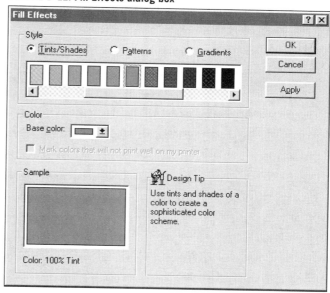

FIGURE D-23: **Formatting applied to objects**

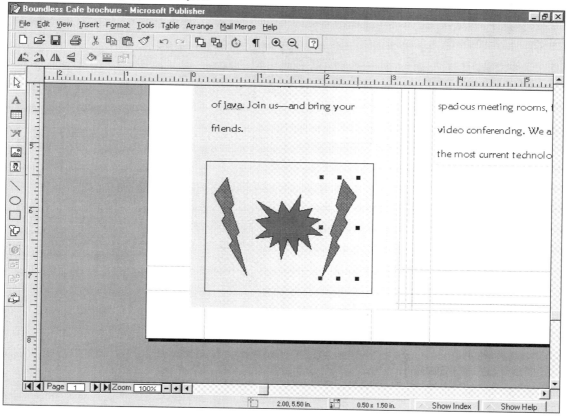

Practice

► Concepts Review

Label each of the elements of the Publisher window shown in Figure D-24.

FIGURE D-24

Bring to front button
1

custom Rotate Button
3

Crop Picture button

Rectangle tool
4

custom Shapes button
5

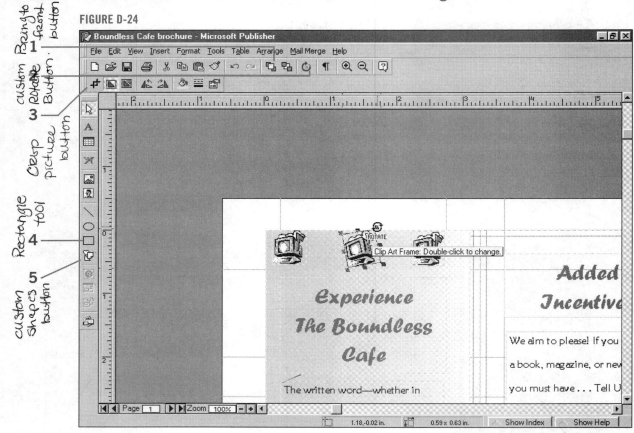

Boundless Cafe brochure - Microsoft Publisher

File Edit View Insert Format Tools Table Arrange Mail Merge Help

Clip Art Frame: Double-click to change.

Experience
The Boundless
Cafe

The written word—whether in

Added
Incentive

We aim to please! If you

a book, magazine, or new

you must have . . . Tell U

Page 1   Zoom 100%

1.18,-0.02 in.   0.59 x 0.63 in.   Show Index   Show Help

Match each of the terms or buttons with the statement that describes its function.

6. Contains clip art ▽
7. Sends an object to the back A
8. Conceals part(s) of images E
9. Brings an object forward C
10. Rotator pointer F
11. Drag to draw a custom shape B

a. [icon]
b. +
c. [icon]
d. Clip Gallery
e. [crop icon] CROP
f. [rotate icon] ROTATE

Select the best answer from the list of choices.

12. Create a square using the Rectangle Tool by holding:
   a. [Ctrl].
   b. [Alt].
   c. [Shift].
   d. [Esc].

13. Each of the following is true about clip art images, *except*:
   a. They can be rotated.
   b. They can be copied.
   c. They can be flipped.
   d. They can be cropped.

14. Which button *cannot* be used with clip art?
   a. [image]
   b. [image]
   c. [image]
   d. [image]

15. Rotate an object in 15-degree increments by holding:
   a. [Ctrl][Shift].
   b. [Alt][Ctrl].
   c. [Alt][Shift].
   d. [Esc].

16. Resize an object while maintaining its scale by holding:
   a. [Shift].
   b. [Alt][Shift].
   c. [Ctrl].
   d. [Alt].

17. Which pointer is used to draw a custom shape?
   a. [image]
   b. [image]
   c. [image]
   d. [image]

18. To create a circle, click the _____ button then press and hold [Shift].
   a. [image]
   b. [image]
   c. [image]
   d. [image]

19. **Which pointer is used to copy an object without placing a copy on the Clipboard?**

    a.

    b. ➤

    c. ➤₊

    d. +

20. **Which button is used to add colors and patterns to objects?**

    a. ⬚

    b. ⬚

    c. ⬚

    d. ⬚

▶ Skills Review

If you complete all of the exercises in this unit, you may run out of space on your Project Disk. To make sure you have enough disk space, please copy files Pub D-2 and Pub D-3 onto a new disk; copy files Pub D-4 and Pub D-5 onto another new disk. Use the new disks to complete the rest of the exercises in this unit.

1. **Insert and resize clip art.**
    a. Start Publisher.
    b. Open the file PUB D-2 and save it on your Project Disk as Lug Nuts promo.
    c. Display pages 2 and 3.
    d. Draw a frame for clip art from 3⅜" V/4¼" H to 4¼" V/5³⁄₁₆" H.
    e. Find artwork in the Clip Gallery containing the keyword "horse". Use the image of the black running horse with the filename horse.wmf. If you do not have this image, use another image of your choice.
    f. Insert the image.
    g. Resize the image to approximately a 1-inch square while maintaining its proportions.
    h. Save your work.

2. **Copy and move an object.**
    a. Move the clip art object to the upper-left corner of page 2, so that the bottom edge is at 1" V and the left edge is at 0".
    b. Copy the image to the Clipboard using the pop-up menu, then use the pop-up menu to paste the object.
    c. Move the newly pasted copy to the right side of the page, so that the bottom edge is at 1" V and the left edge is at 2¼" H.
    d. Use the quick copy pointer to create a third copy and place it between the first and second images. Be sure to release [Ctrl] after releasing the mouse button.
    e. Save your work.

3. **Crop an image.**
    a. Select the nature scene in the center of page 2.
    b. Zoom in to the object.
    c. Click the Crop Picture button on the Formatting toolbar.
    d. Crop the left edge of the image so that the image begins at 1⅛" H.

e. Crop the bottom edge of the image so that the image ends at 2⅜" V.

f. Turn off the cropping pointer.

g. Resize the image while retaining its proportions so that it occupies 1" V/¹³⁄₁₆" H to 2¾" V/2¼" H.

h. Save your work.

4. Align and group artwork.

a. Select all three horse images.

b. Line up the objects using the top edges.

c. Group the objects.

d. Move the object to the bottom of the third page. (*Hint*: The new bottom margin should be 4¼" V.)

e. Ungroup the object.

f. Save the publication.

5. Layer objects.

a. Drag a copy of the center horse so its top-left edge is at 1¾" V/1¾" H.

b. Send the object behind the nature scene.

c. Send the object to the front.

d. Deselect the horse image.

e. Save the publication.

6. Rotate art.

a. Select the horse image in the nature scene.

b. Rotate the image 30 degrees using the mouse pointer.

c. Select the image of the vehicle at the bottom of page 2.

d. Rotate the vehicle 20 degrees.

e. Deselect the vehicle.

f. Save the publication.

7. Use drawing tools.

a. Create a rectangle from roughly 3" V/⅛" H to 4⅛" V/¾" H using the Snap To feature.

b. Zoom in to the rectangle.

c. Draw a right-pointing custom shape (third from the left in the fourth row) at 3½" V/¼" H to 4" V/⅝" H.

d. Click the Flip Vertical button.

e. Save your work.

8. Fill drawn shapes.

a. Change the pattern of the custom shape to a checkerboard (fourth pattern from the left in the patterns list) using its default colors.

b. Change the fill color of the drawn box to gray: the ninth variation of black whose RGB is (178, 178, 178).

c. Save your work.

d. Spell check your work.

e. Print the publication.

▶ Independent Challenges

1. The sandwich shop The Hungry Elf has asked you to create a sign that lists its hours. The client started it, but needs you to make it look more attractive. Use your skills with clip art and drawing tools to make this sign.

To complete this independent challenge:

a. Start Publisher if necessary, open the file PUB D-3, and save it as Hungry Elf sign on your Project Disk.

b. Decrease the size of the existing graphics. (*Hint*: You may have to group multiple objects.)

c. Replace the default text for the business hours.

d. Add ruler guides, if necessary, to help you position new graphic elements.

e. Add a new piece of clip art, or scan in artwork, if possible.

f. If desired, rotate the artwork.

g. Use the drawing tools to create a unique look. Add colors and patterns if necessary.

h. Save the publication.

i. Print the publication.

2. As the top-selling realtor in your firm, Haven Homes, you want your open-house flyers to be dazzling. You have an open house coming up this weekend, and you need to create a flyer.

To complete this independent challenge:

a. Start Publisher, open the file PUB D-4, and save it as 1613 Red Rock flyer on your Project Disk.

b. Replace the placeholder for the photo with suitable clip art, or scan in a photo of a home, if possible.

c. Make up text details about the house.

d. Crop the clip art to best suit your publication.

e. Add objects created with drawing tools, and add color and patterns if appropriate. If necessary, resize any drawn objects.

f. Copy any objects you want repeated in the publication.

g. Apply formatting such as colors and patterns.

h. Save and print the publication.

3. Design a business card for yourself that shows off your Publisher skills and contains attractive artwork.

To complete this independent challenge:

a. Start Publisher if necessary, then use the Catalog to create a business card using any style and design choices you want.

b. Save the publication on your Project Disk as Personal Business Card.

c. Add a picture and/or drawn objects.

d. Arrange the information in an attractive format, using your graphics skills.

e. Layer objects, bringing some to the front and others to the back.

f. Save and print the publication.

4. You have been asked to create a home page for your school. Using your Internet skills, you surf the Net to see home pages for other institutions.
To complete this independent challenge:

a. Log on to the Internet and use your browser to go to http://www.course.com. From there, click Student Online Companions, click the link for the book you are using, then click the Microsoft Publisher link for Unit D.

b. Use each of the sites to get ideas about creating your school's Web site. You can also link to your favorite school to see how its Web site is designed.

c. While connected to the Internet, use your favorite browser to search for other college or university home pages. Take note of the types of graphics they use.

d. Start Publisher, use the Catalog to create a single-page Web site and save it on your Project Disk as College Home Page.

e. Replace the default artwork. If possible, use real photos.

f. Add appropriate text to describe artwork.

g. Format the artwork using your Publisher skills by cropping any undesirable elements from the image, or adding formatting and colors to drawn shapes.

h. Copy and align images to enhance the publication.

i. Save the publication.

j. Spell check your work.

k. Print the publication.

▶ Visual Workshop

Open the file PUB D-5 and save it on your Project Disk as Winston's Designs. Use Figure D-25 as a guide. You can find the replacement clip art by searching for the keyword "gardening". (*Hint:* The image in your file is behind the text box.) Save and print the publication.

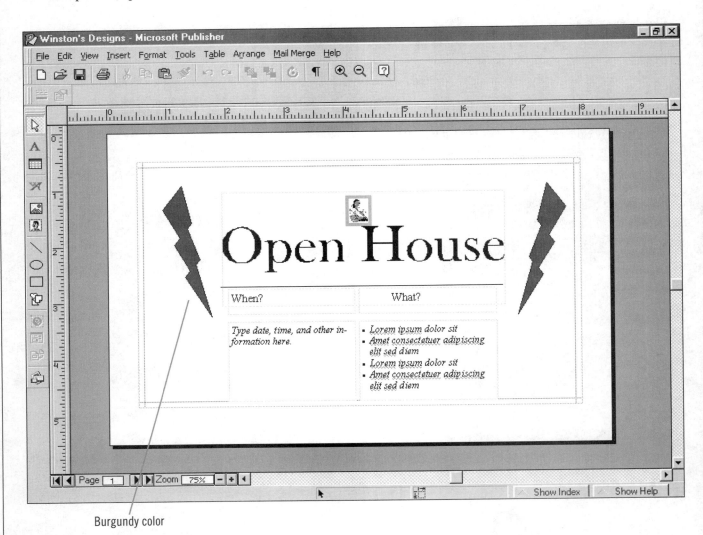

Burgundy color

Enhancing
a Publication

Objectives

- ► **Define styles**
- ► **Modify and apply a style**
- ► **Change a format into a style**
- ► **Create columns**
- ► **Adjust text overflows**
- ► **Add Continued on/from notices**
- ► **Add drop caps**
- ► **Create reversed text**

Text within a publication must be easy to read. Professionals advise you not to use more than two fonts per page because too many fonts make a page look busy and detract from the publication's message. Formatting a limited number of fonts in different sizes, with bold or italics, can add to the visual interest without creating a confusing array of fonts. Story text can be in one or more columns, depending on the desired layout. Any text not fitting in a single text frame on a page can be continued elsewhere within the publication. Publisher has tools to help map and link the frames to create a cohesive publication. Steve Kelly is an account representative for *Titanic News*, for which Image Masters creates a monthly newsletter. He is working on the text for the first issue.

Defining Styles

The appearance of text in a publication determines its legibility. Text that is too large looks awkward; text that is too small or fancy looks busy and can be hard to read. You can easily provide consistency within the text by using styles. A **style** is a defined set of text formatting attributes, such as a font, font size, and paragraph alignment. Creating a style means that all the text in a publication can have a consistent look. ◢◣◤ Steve opens the newsletter he started earlier and defines a style that he will use throughout the publication.

Steps 1 2 3 4

1. Before you start this unit, copy the files **PUB E-1** and **PUB E-2** from your Project Disk to a new blank formatted disk

2. Start Publisher, open the file **PUB E-1**, click **OK** to initialize your printer, click **Yes** to update all embedded objects if necessary, then save the file as **Titanic News**
   You open the Text Style dialog box to see the existing styles.

Trouble?

If the You've Chosen a Text Styles Option step-by-step dialog box opens, click Continue.

3. Click **Format** on the menu bar, then click **Text Style**
   The Text Style dialog box opens, as shown in Figure E-1. This dialog box lets you modify existing styles and create new ones. You want to create a style that can be used in other paragraphs in this publication.

4. Click the **Create a new style button** >
   The Create New Style dialog box opens, as shown in Figure E-2. You want the point size of the font to be 12 and the alignment to be center.

5. Click the **Character type and size button** >, click the **Size list arrow**, click **12**, then click **OK**
   Now you change the alignment of text within the paragraph.

6. Click the **Indents and lists button** >, click the **Alignment list arrow**, click **Center**, then click **OK**
   The sample in the Create New Style dialog box displays the changes. Once the formatting attributes have been changed, you give the style a name.

7. Type **Titanic paragraph** in the Enter new style name text box, then click **OK**
   The new style appears in the list of existing styles, as shown in Figure E-3.

8. Click **Close**
   Now the style can be applied to text in the publication. You save your work.

9. Click the **Save button** 🖫 on the Standard toolbar

FIGURE E-1: **Text Style dialog box**

Available styles —————
appear here

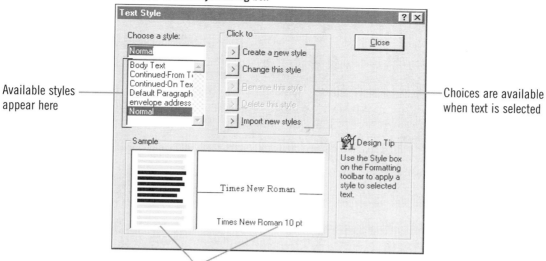

————— Choices are available
when text is selected

Sample of currently selected style

FIGURE E-2: **Create New Style dialog box**

Click here to —————
modify attributes

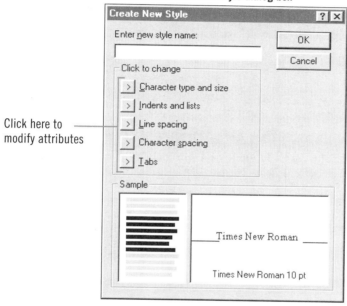

FIGURE E-3: **New style in Text Style dialog box**

New style —————

New alignment —————

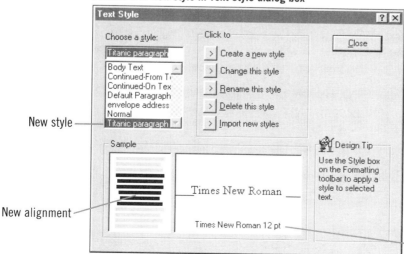

————— New point size

Modifying and Applying a Style

Since any style can be modified, you have the freedom to change the appearance of selected text assigned to a specific style with ease. If you decide to change a style, you can reapply the modified style to reformat text. Once you've defined a style, you can apply it to give the text those attributes. ✎ Steve wants to modify the style he just created. Then, he'll insert a Word document and apply the defined style to it.

Steps 1234

1. **Click Format on the menu bar, then click Text Style**
   Titanic paragraph, the style you created, is in the list of styles. You want to change the font size from 12 point to 10 point and return to full justification.

2. **Click Titanic paragraph from the Choose a style list, then click the Change this style button ⟩**
   The Change Style dialog box opens. You want to change the point size and the alignment.

3. **Click the Character type and size button ⟩, click the Size list arrow, click 10, then click OK**
   Next, you change the alignment to justified because you want new text to look consistent with text already in the publication.

4. **Click the Indents and lists button ⟩, click the Alignment list arrow, click Justified, click OK, then click OK to close the Change Style dialog box**
   The modified text size should display in the Text Style dialog box, as shown in Figure E-4.

5. **Click Close to close the Text Style dialog box**
   Now, you zoom in to where you will insert a Word file.

6. **Click the text frame at 4" V/7" H, then click the Zoom In button ⊞ twice on the horizontal scroll bar so you can see both the top and bottom of the text frame**
   The zoom percentage will differ with different-size monitors. Now, you insert a Word file.

> **Trouble?**
> To turn the Connect Frames toolbar on, click Tools on the menu bar, then click Text Frame Connecting.

7. **Right-click the text frame, point to Change text, click Text File, click PUB E-2 from the new disk, click OK, then click No in the warning box to not use autoflow**
   Using the autoflow feature automatically takes text that doesn't fit in a frame and places it in the next available text frame. Compare your page to Figure E-5. The inserted text is in the Arial font at 12 point size. Now you want to apply the modified Titanic paragraph style to this text.

8. **Right-click the text frame, point to Change text, then click Highlight Entire Story**
   The Font and Font Size text boxes become blank, indicating that more than one font and size are selected. Once the text is selected, you can apply the style.

9. **Click the Style list arrow on the Formatting toolbar, then click Titanic paragraph**
   Compare your page to Figure E-6. The text is now Times New Roman, 10 point, and justified.

10. **Click the Zoom Out button ⊟ twice, then save your publication**

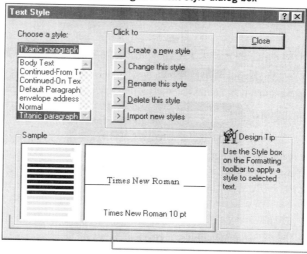

FIGURE E-4: **Text size changed in Text Style dialog box**

New style attributes display here

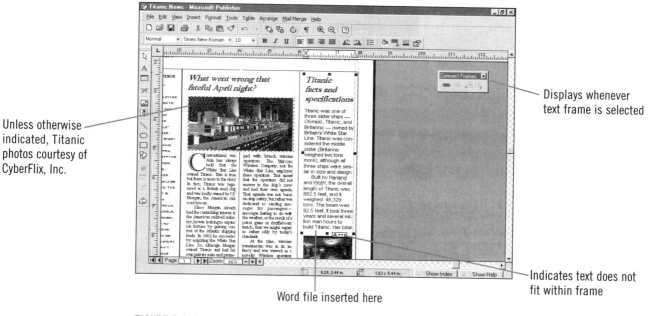

FIGURE E-5: **Word file inserted into text frame**

Displays whenever text frame is selected

Unless otherwise indicated, Titanic photos courtesy of CyberFlix, Inc.

Indicates text does not fit within frame

Word file inserted here

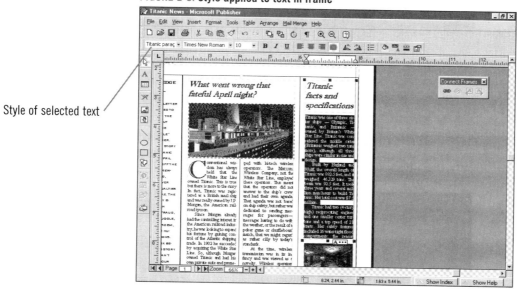

FIGURE E-6: **Style applied to text in frame**

Style of selected text

Changing a Format into a Style

A style can be created from formatted text within a text frame. This means that without knowing all the attributes that make up text appearance, you can turn it into a style. This process is called creating a **style by example**. A format is changed into a style by typing a name in the Style list box on the Formatting toolbar. Creating a style by example makes the style available for use over and over again in the publication. The difference between using a style or using the Format painter is that the Format painter button reformats selected characters based on the style of currently selected characters, but does not store or name the style. Steve likes the way the story titles appear and wants to create a style from this format that he can use throughout the publication.

Steps

1. Click anywhere within the What went wrong that fateful April night? heading beneath the newsletter masthead, then press [F9]
   You want to create a style from this format.

2. Click within the Style list box on the Formatting toolbar
   The current style—in this case, Normal—becomes selected, as shown in Figure E-7. To create a style from the current formatting, you type a name in the Style list box.

3. Type Titanic heading in the Style list box, then press [Enter]
   The Create Style By Example dialog box opens, as shown in Figure E-8. The Sample box shows you the current style's font and size, as well as its alignment setting. You want to create this style using the formatting of the selected text in the What went wrong that fateful April night? heading.

4. Click OK
   The Create Style By Example dialog box closes. Notice that the new name, Titanic heading, appears in the Style list box, as shown in Figure E-9. You decide to zoom out.

5. Press [F9]
   You can now use this style elsewhere in the publication. Now, you save your work.

6. Click the Save button 🖫 on the Standard toolbar

FIGURE E-7: Style selected in the Style list box

Style list box

Selected text frame

FIGURE E-8: Create Style By Example dialog box

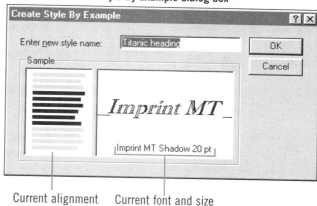

Current alignment   Current font and size

FIGURE E-9: New style name displays in Style list box

New style name

Adjusting spaces between characters

Sometimes characters don't look quite right when they're printed: they may seem packed too close together or spread too far apart. Adjusting the spacing between character pairs, or **kerning**, can make text look better. The characters A W R Y might have more space between the letters A, W, R, and Y than you want. You can kern these characters so there is less space between the characters, so that it now looks this way—AWRY. Publisher automatically kerns characters having point sizes greater than 14, but you can kern any characters you choose by selecting the character pair(s) to be adjusted, clicking Format on the menu bar, then clicking Character Spacing. You can change scaling, tracking, and kerning of characters using the Character Spacing dialog box shown in Figure E-10.

FIGURE E-10: Character Spacing dialog box

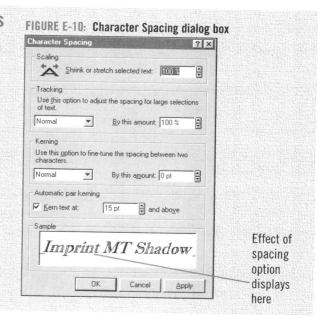

Effect of spacing option displays here

Creating Columns

When a text frame is created, it contains a single column. Most newsletter stories are formatted in multiple columns to give a more professional look. Multiple columns of equal widths that allow text to flow from one column to the next can be created within a single frame, or multiple text frames can be created and placed adjacent to one another to give the appearance of columns. You can create multiple columns within a single text frame by changing the frame's properties. Steve wants to create four columns within a single text frame on page 4. The text in these columns will surround a graphic image.

1. Click the Last Page button ▶| on the horizontal scroll bar
You create a single text frame to fill the space beneath the Secondary Article heading. Use the Snap To guides on the Tools menu and zoom when necessary to create frames.

2. Click the Text Frame Tool [A] on the Objects toolbar, drag the ✛ pointer from 6¾" V/¾" H to 10" V/7½" H, then zoom in if necessary
The single-column text frame appears and is selected; the graphic image is hidden beneath the text frame, as shown in Figure E-11. You want to change the text frame's properties to create four columns with a margin between the columns.

3. Right-click the text frame, point to Change Frame, then click Text Frame Properties
The Text Frame Properties dialog box opens, as shown in Figure E-12. You want to change this single-column text to four columns.

4. Double-click the Columns Number box, then type 4
It's important that columns have a cushion of white space between them. Without white space, the page will appear cluttered and the story will be difficult to read.

5. Click the Columns Spacing up arrow twice to display .28", then click OK
The dialog box closes, displaying the text frame with four columns. Now you want to send the text frame back so that the graphic image will appear in the foreground.

6. Click the Send to Back button 🔳 on the Standard toolbar
The graphic image appears in the foreground. When you type or insert text, it will wrap around the image in either a rectangular shape or closely hugging the image. Compare your publication with Figure E-13. Save your work.

7. Press [F9], then click the Save button 🔳 on the Standard toolbar

FIGURE E-11: **Single-column text frame**

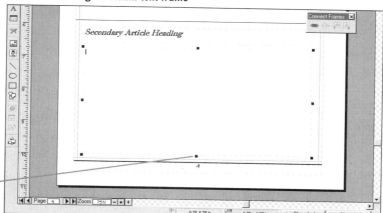

Single-column text frame
obscures graphic image

FIGURE E-12: **Text Frame Properties dialog box**

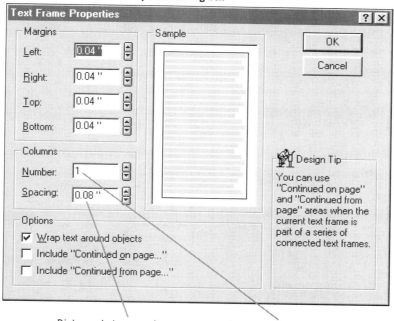

Distance between columns   Indicate the number of columns here

FIGURE E-13: **Four columns created with graphic image in foreground**

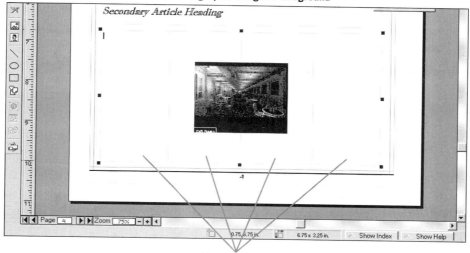

Four columns

Adjusting Text Overflows

Text does not always fit neatly within a text frame on one page. In some situations, such as a newsletter, you may want to have more than one story begin on one page and continue on others. Publisher makes it easy to take the overflow from one text frame and pour it into another text frame using the Connect button at the bottom of the frame. A series of helpful pointers determine how and where you distribute the text throughout the frames in the publication. Various buttons and pointers help identify and navigate connected frames. Steve wants to place the overflow text from a story on page 1 into text on pages 2 and 3.

Steps 1 2 3 4

QuickTip

Break a link between connected frames by clicking ⊗.

1. **Click the First Page button ◄| on the horizontal scroll bar, then click the text frame at 4" V/7" H**
   The Connect Frames button [A • • •] at the bottom of the frame indicates that there is overflow text. Text that does not fit in this frame can be continued—using the 🫗 and 🫗 pointers—in other text frames. Frames that have text poured into them are linked to the previous frame, indicated by the [⟵≡] button. You want to pour this text into the frame on page 2.

2. **Click the Connect Text Frame button ⊜ on the Connect Frames toolbar, as shown in Figure E-14**
   The pointer changes to 🫗. This is the pitcher of text that you will pour into the next frame. When you place this pitcher over a text frame, it changes to a pouring pitcher 🫗, indicating that you can pour the text into the frame. You want the overflow to begin pouring on page 2.

Trouble?

If tippages appear, press [Esc] to turn them off.

3. **Click the Next Page button ▶| on the horizontal scroll bar, position the pointer at 2" V/1" H, then click the frame with the pouring pitcher pointer 🫗**
   Compare your page to Figure E-15. The overflow text is poured into the text frame, and the Connect Frames button indicates there is still more overflow. You want to view pages 2 and 3.

4. **Click View on the menu bar, then click Two-Page Spread**
   Pages 2 and 3 are both visible. You want to pour the overflow from page 2 into the text frame on page 3. When you pour the overflow text, a Go To Next Frame button [≡ →] will display at the bottom of the text frame on page 2.

QuickTip

Clicking the Go To Previous Frame button is a fast way to jump to the previous connecting frame.

5. **Click ⊜, the pointer changes to 🫗, then click 🫗 on page 3 at 8" V/13" H**
   Compare your work to Figure E-16. The overflow text from page 2 displays on page 3. The Go To Previous Frame button [← ≡] displays at the top of the text frame. You want to save your work.

6. **Click the Save button 🖫 on the Standard toolbar**
   You want to read the text that you have been inserting into the newsletter. You display page 1, then select and zoom into the beginning of the story so you can read it.

7. **Click ◄|, click the text frame at 4" V/7" H, then press [F9]**
   You read the displayed story, then use the Go To Frame buttons to read the entire story.

8. **Click [≡ →] on pages 2 and 3, using the Zoom feature where necessary**
   When you have finished reading the stories, you zoom out and save your work.

9. **Press [F9], then click 🖫**

FIGURE E-14: **Preparing to click the Connect Frames button**

Object position coordinates

FIGURE E-15: **Overflow text poured into frame**

Go To Previous
Frame button

Indicates
more overflow
text

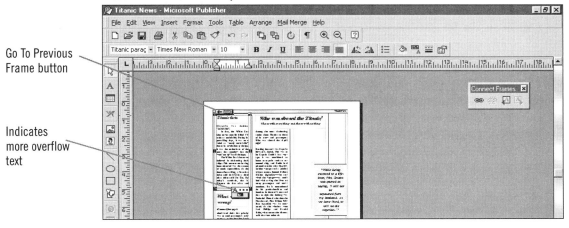

FIGURE E-16: **Completion of overflow text**

Indicates linked
frames

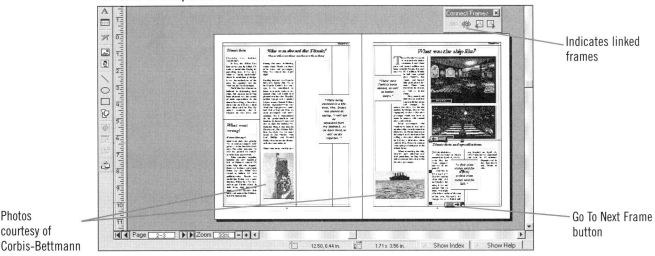

Photos
courtesy of
Corbis-Bettmann

Go To Next Frame
button

Adding Continued on/from Notices

When it is not possible to start and finish a story on the same page, continued notices can be added. Sometimes, publications are specifically designed with stories spanning several pages to encourage readers to see all the pages in the entire publication. Because you want it to be as easy as possible to find and read all segments of a story, Publisher makes it easy to create **Continued on** and **Continued from** notices. These notices automatically insert text with the correct page reference—and references automatically update if you move the text frame. Steve wants to insert Continued on and Continued from notices in the story that spans several pages. He returns to page 1, the beginning of the story.

Steps

1. Click the First Page button on the horizontal scroll bar, click the text frame on page 1 at 4" V/7" H, press [F9], then scroll down so the bottom of the text frame is visible
   The text frame is enlarged. You want the first Continued on notice to appear at the bottom of this text frame since the text continues on page 2. Create a Continued on notice by modifying the text frame's properties.

2. Click Format on the menu bar, then click Text Frame Properties
   The Text Frame Properties dialog box opens, as shown in Figure E-17. Clicking check boxes in the Text Frame Properties dialog box creates Continued on/Continued from notices.

   Trouble?
   Continued on/from notices display only if they refer to text on pages other than the current page.

3. Click the Include "Continued on page..." check box, then click OK
   Compare your page to Figure E-18. You want to insert a Continued from notice at the beginning of the story on page 2. Since this page contains a single text frame, you can insert the Continued on and Continued from notices at the same time.

4. Press [F9], then click the Go to Next Frame button
   The beginning of the story on page 2 displays. Again, you open the Text Properties dialog box.

   QuickTip
   Continued on/from notices must be turned on for each text frame. A single text frame containing multiple columns can turn on both notices in one step.

5. Right-click the selected text frame, point to Change Frame, click Text Frame Properties, click the Include "Continued on page..." check box, click the Include "Continued from page..." check box, then click OK
   Both notices display at the beginning and end of the text frame. You add a Continued from notice at the beginning of the text frame on page 3.

6. Click on page 2

7. Right-click the selected text frame on page 3, point to Change Frame, click Text Frame Properties, click the "Continued from page ..." check box, then click OK
   The Continued from notice displays. You want to see the notice, so you zoom in.

   Trouble?
   Consider that Continued on/from notices make a story take up more space on a page, adding several lines to its length.

8. Press [F9]
   Compare your screen with Figure E-19. Satisfied with your work, you zoom out and save the publication.

9. Press [F9], then click the Save button on the Standard toolbar

FIGURE E-17: Text Frame Properties dialog box

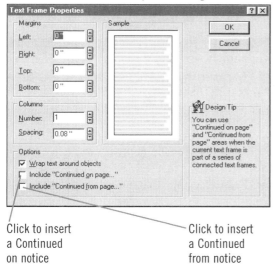

Click to insert a Continued on notice

Click to insert a Continued from notice

FIGURE E-18: Continued on notice

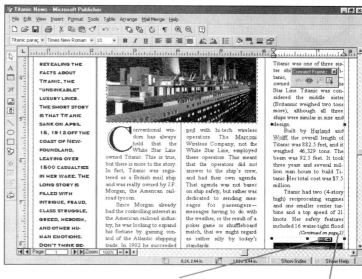

Click to go to the next frame

Notice automatically cites the correct page

FIGURE E-19: Continued from notice

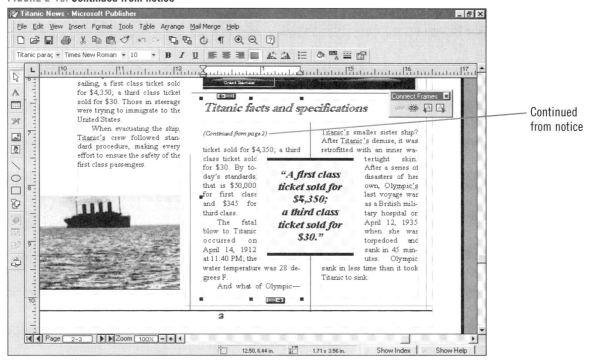

Continued from notice

(Continued from page 2)

"A first class ticket sold for $4,350; a third class ticket sold for $30."

Changing the appearance of continued notices

If the appearance of a Continued on or Continued from notice does not appeal to you, it can be changed. Each type of continued notice has a defined style—you can see the style name in the Style list box. Change the style of a continued notice by selecting the notice you want to change, making formatting modifications, clicking the style name in the Style list box, then pressing [Enter]. You can also use the Change Style dialog box to change the continued notice style.

Publisher 98

Adding Drop Caps

In addition to using defined styles to give stories a consistent look, you can also add **drop caps**, a fancy first letter at the beginning of each paragraph or story. A drop cap can occur wherever you choose: at the beginning of each paragraph in a story, or only at the beginning of the story. Publisher lets you choose from defined character types that use different fonts and line heights, or you can create your own. ▰▰▰ Steve wants to dress up several stories using drop caps. He starts by applying a predefined fancy letter to the story he just worked on.

1. Click the **First Page button** ◀ on the horizontal scroll bar, click the **text frame on page 1** at **4" V/7" H**, then click anywhere in the first paragraph
   Apply a fancy letter to the initial character in the first paragraph.

2. Click **Format** on the menu bar, then click **Drop Cap**
   The Drop Cap dialog box opens. You decide to use the largest letter in the same font as the headline.

QuickTip

The default font for the drop cap is the same as the font in the selected story.

3. Click the **drop cap style** shown in Figure E-20, then click **OK**
   The selected drop cap appears as the first letter of the first paragraph. You want to add drop caps to a story on page 2, but because the text almost fills the text frame, you choose a custom first letter so you can adjust the character's height.

4. Click the **Next Page button** ▶ on the horizontal scroll bar
   Now you highlight the entire story and open the Drop Cap dialog box.

5. Right-click the **textbox** at **4" V/4" H**, point to **Change Text**, click **Highlight Entire Story**, click **Format** on the menu bar, then click **Drop Cap**
   You want to create a custom first letter using the Drop Cap dialog box.

Trouble?

Drop caps add to the length of a story.

6. Click the **Custom Drop Cap tab**
   You begin customizing the first-letter settings. You want a dropped letter that is two lines high.

7. Click the **Dropped letter position**, double-click the **Size of letters text box**, type **2**, as shown in Figure E-21, click **OK**, then click the **scratch area**
   The customized first letter is added throughout the story. You view the story to see the drop caps. Compare you work to Figure E-22. Save your work with your modifications.

8. Click the **Save button** 🖫 on the Standard toolbar

FIGURE E-20: **Drop Cap dialog box**

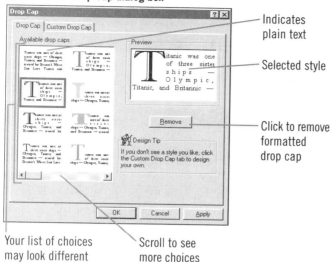

Indicates plain text

Selected style

Click to remove formatted drop cap

Your list of choices may look different

Scroll to see more choices

FIGURE E-21: **Creating a custom drop cap**

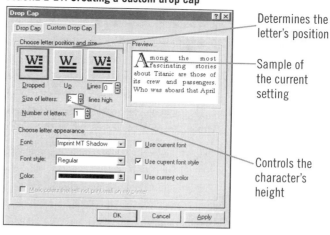

Determines the letter's position

Sample of the current setting

Controls the character's height

Drop caps added

FIGURE E-22: **Drop caps added**

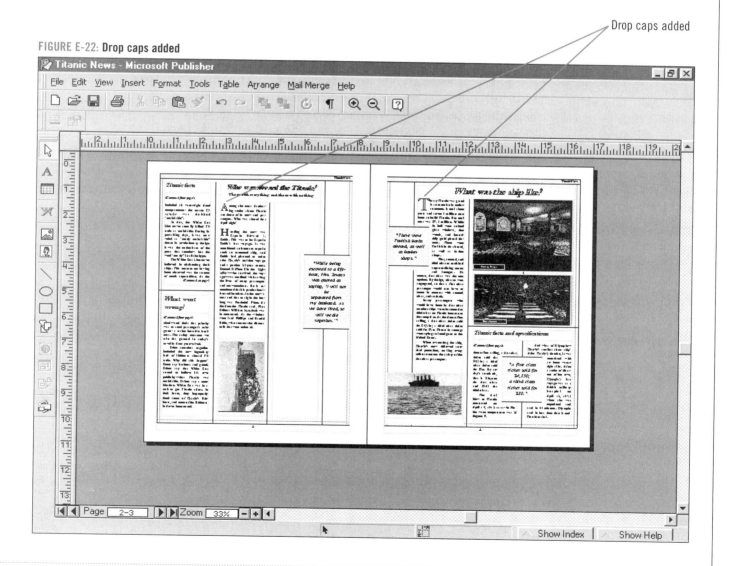

Publisher 98

Creating Reversed Text

Another way to add emphasis to text—particularly titles—is to create reversed text. Reversed text displays as light characters on a dark background. This format makes the text look as though it was cut out of the background. This effect is created by selecting all the text within the title's frame, then using buttons on the Formatting toolbar to change the colors of the font and the object. Steve wants to create the effect of reversed text in the sidebar on the first page.

1. Click the First Page button ◄| on the horizontal scroll bar
   The first page displays. Next, you select the sidebar and zoom in.

2. Click the frame at 4" V/1" H, then press [F9]
   The sidebar is selected and enlarged. You use the keyboard shortcut to select all the text within the frame.

3. Press [Ctrl][A]
   The text is selected, as shown in Figure E-23. Next, you change the font color.

4. Click the Font Color button 🅰 on the Formatting toolbar, then click the Accent5 (White) color box
   The text in the frame seems to disappear. When creating reverse text, the order in which you change the font color or object color doesn't matter. Regardless of the order, at some point they will both be the same color. Now you change the fill color of the object.

QuickTip

Remember that when objects are selected, everything displays as if reversed.

5. Click the Fill Color button ◇ on the Formatting toolbar, then click the Main (Black) color box
   The object's background changes to black. You deselect the text frame so you can see the reversed text.

6. Click outside the text frame
   You compare your work to Figure E-24, then you zoom out and spell check your publication.

7. Press [F9], then spell check your publication
   You save your work and print the publication.

8. Click the Save button 💾 on the Standard toolbar, then click the Print button 🖨

9. Click File on the menu bar, then click Exit

In reverse, this text will look as it does when it's selected

Practice

► Concepts Review

Label each of the elements of the Publisher window shown in Figure E-25.

FIGURE E-25   *(handwritten labels:)* STYLE LIST BOX 1   GoTo previous 2 Frame 3 Button   SEND TO BACK Button 4   5 FILL Color Button   6 InDiCATes LinkeD Frames   DROPCAP

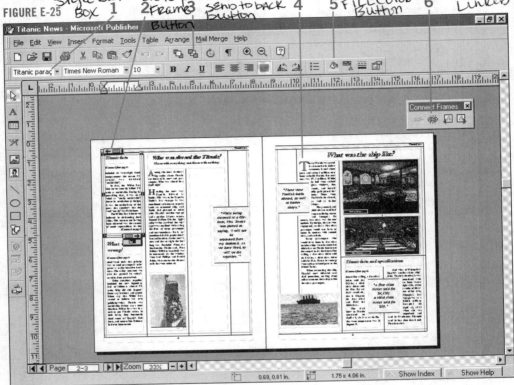

Match each of the buttons and pointers with the statement that describes its function.

7. Pouring pointer E
8. Pitcher pointer C
9. Go to Next Frame button F
10. Link Frames button B
11. Go to Previous Frame button D
12. Connect Text Frames button A

a. [image]
b. [image]
c. [image]
d. [image]
e. [image]
f. [image]

Select the best answer from the list of choices.

13. Select the entire contents of a frame by pressing:
    a. [Shift][A].
    b. [Alt][A].
    c. [Ctrl][A].
    d. [Esc][A].

14. Prepare to pour overflow text by clicking the Connect Frame button when the pointer looks like:
   a.
   b.
   c.
   d.

15. Which button takes you to the next frame?
   a.
   b.
   c.
   d.

16. Which button indicates the existence of overflow text?
   a.
   b.
   c.
   d.

17. Which dialog box is used to create Continued on/from notices?
   a. Continued Notices
   b. Notices
   c. Frame Properties
   d. Text Frame Properties

18. Changing a format into a style is called:
   a. Format stylization.
   b. Creating a style by example.
   c. Stylizing a format.
   d. Creating a format master.

19. Which pointer is used to pour overflow text into a text frame?
   a.
   b.
   c.
   d.

20. Adjusting the spaces between characters is called:
   a. Spacing.
   b. Kerning.
   c. Carning.
   d. Adjusting.

21. **Which dialog box controls the number of columns in a text frame?**
    a. Text Frame Characteristics
    b. Columns in Text Frame
    c. Modify Columns
    d. Text Frame Properties
22. **Which dialog box adds/removes a drop cap?**
    a. Drop Cap
    b. Text Frame Properties
    c. Fancy First Letter
    d. Spacing Between Characters

▶ Skills Review

If you complete all of the exercises in this unit, you may run out of space on your Project Disk. To make sure you have enough disk space, please copy the files PUB E-3 and PUB E-4 to a separate blank formatted disk, then copy the files PUB E-5, PUB E-6, and PUB E-7 to another blank formatted disk.

Throughout these exercises, use the zoom feature where necessary.

1. **Define styles.**
   a. Start Publisher.
   b. Open the file PUB E-3, initialize your printer, and update all embedded objects if necessary.
   c. Save the file on your Project Disk as Titanic Sampler.
   d. Create a new text style that is 20 point Copperplate Gothic Bold font.
   e. Name this new style Feature heading.
   f. Save your work.
2. **Modify and apply a style.**
   a. Change the font size of the Feature heading style to 22 points.
   b. Change the font color of the Feature heading style to Periwinkle.
   c. Display page 2 of the publication.
   d. Apply the Feature heading style to the "What was the ship like?" heading.
   e. Save your work.
3. **Change a format into a style.**
   a. Select the "Who was on board Titanic?" text frame on page 2.
   b. Using the Style list box create a style called "About Passengers" that uses the settings in the "Who was on board Titanic?" heading.
   c. Apply the About Passengers style to the "Who was on board Titanic" text frame on page 1.
   d. Save your work.
4. **Create columns.**
   a. Display page 2.
   b. Using the Text Frame Tool, draw a text frame beneath the "What was the ship like?" heading from 5¾" V/⅝" H to 10⅛" V/6⅛" H.
   c. Create four columns in this text frame with .28" spacing between columns.
   d. Send the text frame to the back.
   e. Insert the Word file PUB E-4; do not use autoflow.
   f. Save the publication.

5. **Adjust text overflows.**
   a. Select the text frame beneath the "Who was on board Titanic?" heading on page 1.
   b. Using the Connect Frames button, pour the text into each of the remaining text frames on page 1.
   c. Pour the text from the fourth column on page 1 into each of the four columns on the top of page 2.
   d. Save the publication.

6. **Add Continued on/from notices.**
   a. Add a Continued on notice on the fourth column text frame in the "Who was on board Titanic?" story on page 1.
   b. Add a Continued from notice in the first column of the "Who was on board Titanic?" story on page 2.
   c. Save the publication.

7. **Add drop caps.**
   a. Highlight the entire "Who was on board Titanic?" story.
   b. Create a dropped custom first letter 2 lines high using the Lucida Sans font.
   c. Save your work.

8. **Create reversed text.**
   a. Select the entire contents of the "What was the ship like?" text frame on page 2.
   b. Change the font color to turquoise.
   c. Change the fill color to blue.
   d. Save your work.
   e. Spell check all the stories in the publication.
   f. Read the stories on the screen.
   g. Print the publication.
   h. Exit Publisher.

▶ Independent Challenges

1. Four-Wheel Giants, a local outdoor driving club, has hired you to create a sign promoting the grand opening of its new driving track. You've started the sign, but it still needs some finishing touches.
   To complete this independent challenge:

   a. Start Publisher if necessary, open the file PUB E-5, and save it as 4-Wheel Giants on your Project Disk.
   b. Create a style for the text frame (announcing the grand opening) on page 2 using any fonts available on your computer.
   c. Pour the text now in the frame on page 1 into the remaining text frames.
   d. Use drop caps to make the text more attractive, making sure the text fits within the frame.
   e. Add Continued on/from notices on pages 1 and 2, making sure the text fits within the frame.
   f. Save the publication.
   g. Read the publication, then spell check it.
   h. Print the publication.

2. In an effort to educate the community, your real estate company is holding a seminar to educate first-time home-buyers in what procedures they should follow and what they can expect. Complete this flyer.

To complete this independent challenge:

a. Start Publisher if necessary, open the file PUB E-6, and save it as Real Estate Seminar on your Project Disk.

b. Pour the text in the top right frame into the frame beneath it.

c. Make all the text within the flyer as attractive as possible.

d. Add drop caps to make the text more attractive.

e. Spell check and read the stories.

f. Save and print the publication.

3. A local pet shop has hired you to design a flyer advertising a contest at your town's annual pet show. The contest is new this year and you want to boost attendance, so you will be offering prizes within the categories.

To complete this independent challenge:

a. Start Publisher if necessary, then use the Catalog to create a contest flyer for the Best Friends pet shop.

b. Save the publication on your Project Disk as Best Friends flyer.

c. Add any artwork or drawn objects that you feel will add to the flyer.

d. Create styles for headings and text.

e. Add drop caps and reversed text to emphasize text.

f. Arrange the information in an attractive format, using your graphics skills.

g. Check spelling, read the stories, then save and print the publication.

4. Your company, Widgets Galore, has asked you to create a home page that customers can use to read your annual report. Surf the Internet to find examples of other corporate home pages, then use the Catalog to create your own.

To complete this independent challenge:

a. Log on to the Internet and use your browser to go to http://www.course.com. From there, click the link Student Online Companions, click Microsoft Publisher 98—Illustrated Introductory, then click the links for Unit E.

b. Use each of the sites to get ideas on creating a corporate Web site.

c. Start Publisher if necessary, use the Catalog to create a corporate Web site, and save it on your Project Disk as Widgets Galore Home Page.

d. Replace the default artwork if possible.

e. Create appropriate text to describe the company.

f. Create text styles for body text and headings. Use these styles throughout your pages.

g. Add drop caps, continued notices, and columns.

h. Save the publication.

i. Spell check and read the stories.

j. Print the publication.

▶ Visual Workshop

Open the file PUB E-7 and save it on your Project Disk as Art Program. Modify this publication so that it looks like Figure E-26, using drop caps, font color, object background color, and text overflows. Save and print the publication.

FIGURE E-26

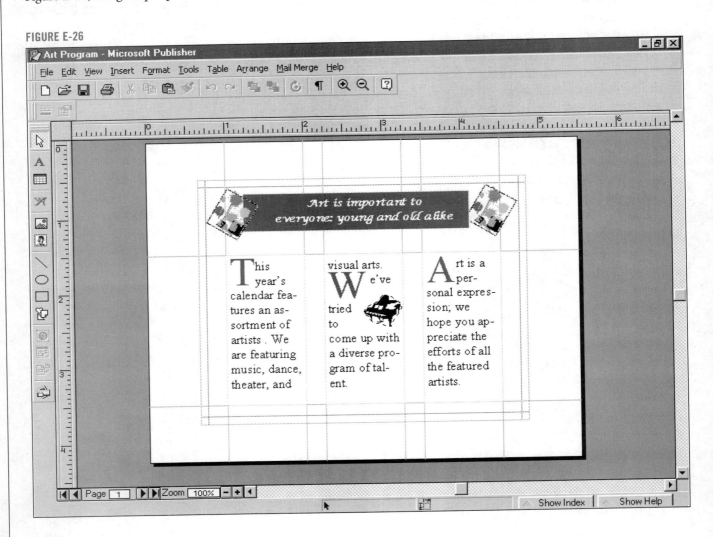

Publisher 98

Unit F

Working
with Multiple Pages

Objectives

- ► Add a page
- ► Delete a page
- ► Work with a background
- ► Create a header and footer
- ► Add page numbers
- ► Work with stories
- ► Use tabs
- ► Create a booklet

Some publications, such as flyers, business cards, or signs, have to be designed as a single page; however, many publications have multiple pages. Publisher makes it easy to add, copy, and delete pages. For a more professional look, repetitive text, such as a title, can be displayed in the same location on the top or bottom of each page. Page numbers and a table of contents can be added to help readers find specific stories. Lisa Morrow, who works with Vintage Homes Real Estate, is working on a publication that lists and describes homes to be viewed at an upcoming open house. The publication is in progress and she needs to add elements common to a multiple-page document.

Adding a Page

Pages can be added to a publication. Depending on how your publication is laid out, you might want to add pages in multiples of 2, although you can add pages one at a time. If existing pages have layout guides or other information in the background, these items will automatically be added to the new pages. You also have the option to copy the objects on any page to a newly inserted page. ◄━━ Lisa opens the publication that contains the information on the open house. She determines that there are more listings for this week and estimates that this publication needs an additional page.

1. Before you start this unit, copy the files PUB F-1 and Vh-logo from your Project Disk to a new blank formatted disk

2. Start Publisher, open the Existing Publication file PUB F-1, click OK to initialize your printer, click Yes to update embedded objects if necessary, then save the file as VH-Open Houses
   Review the publication to see each of the four pages.

3. Click the Next Page button ▶ on the horizontal scroll bar, view the second page, click ▶ slowly two times, then click the First Page button ◄|
   Any number of pages can be added either before or after the current page. To retain a consistent design, you can also choose to duplicate objects—such as text or picture frames—from any specific page. You want to insert the new page after page 2.

4. Click ▶
   Page 2 displays. The pages in this publication contain decorative lines at the top and bottom of each page. You want the new page to include these decorative lines as well.

5. Click Insert on the menu bar, then click Page
   The Insert Page dialog box opens, as shown in Figure F-1. You want to add one new page after the current page (the default value and placement) and duplicate the objects that are on page 2. You can delete the pictures of homes later. The current page is also the default value for duplicating objects.

QuickTip

Move a page by inserting a new page and duplicating the objects from the page you want moved, then deleting the original page.

6. Verify that 1 is in the Number of new pages text box, click the Duplicate all objects on page option button, verify that page 2 is in the text box, then click OK
   Page 3—the new page—displays with the objects on the top and bottom of the page. See Figure F-2. Although you can't tell how many pages there are just by looking at the status bar, you can click the Last Page button to verify that just one page has been added.

7. Click the Last Page button ▶| on the horizontal scroll bar
   Page 5 displays. You return to page 3.

8. Click the Change Pages button [Page ☐] on the horizontal scroll bar
   The Go To Page dialog box opens, as shown in Figure F-3, informing you of the number of pages in your publication and the starting and ending page numbers. You can go to any page in the publication using this dialog box. You want to display the new page, so you type that page number in the text box.

9. Type 3, click OK, then save your work
   Page 3 displays.

FIGURE F-1: **Insert Page dialog box**

Indicate where new page(s) should be inserted

Click to copy objects from a specific page

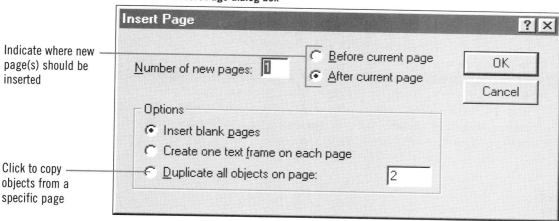

FIGURE F-2: **New page displayed**

Layout guides are added to new page

Duplicated objects

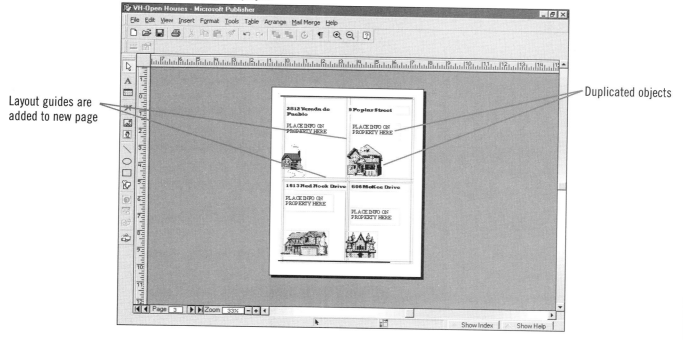

FIGURE F-3: **Go To Page dialog box**

The current page number is automatically displayed

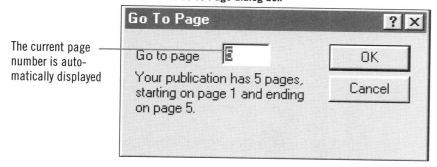

Deleting a Page

Pages that are no longer needed in a publication can be deleted. As a safety measure, Publisher has been designed so that you must be viewing the page that you are deleting. When you delete a page, any objects on that page—as well as the page itself—are deleted from the publication. Any Continued on/Continued from notices are automatically recalculated, and text in a connected frame is moved to the closest available frame on the next page. ⬛ Based on recent information from a Vintage Homes representative, Lisa has determined that she needs to delete one page from the publication. Page 3, which is identical to page 2, is displayed, so she deletes this duplicate page.

1. **Click Edit on the menu bar, then click Delete Page**
   The warning box, shown in Figure F-4, displays. If you did not want to delete this page, you would click Cancel. However, you want to delete this page.

   QuickTip

   If you delete a page in error, immediately click the Undo button 🔄 on the Standard toolbar.

2. **Click OK**
   The Change Pages button indicates that page 3 is displayed. Each time you delete a single page, the Change Pages button will not appear to have changed, even though the displayed page is different. You want to verify that one page has been deleted, and that you now have a four-page publication.

3. **Click the Change Pages button** ▭Page ▭ **on the horizontal scroll bar**
   You can see that your publication now has four pages, starting on page 1 and ending on page 4.

4. **Type 4, then click OK**
   The last page—page 4—displays, as shown in Figure F-5. Return to page 2 since you will be working here next.

5. **Click the Previous Page button** ◀ **on the horizontal scroll bar twice**
   You decide to change from a single page view to a two-page spread so you can see pages 2 and 3 at once.

6. **Click View on the menu bar, then click Two-Page Spread**
   Compare your screen to Figure F-6. You are viewing pages 2 and 3. You save your work.

7. **Click the Save button** 💾 **on the Standard toolbar**

Saving objects on a page

When a page is deleted, all the objects on that page are also deleted. What if you want to save some of those objects for later use? Any objects can be pulled onto the **scratch area**, the gray area surrounding the page in the workspace. Objects in the scratch area are saved along with the publication and can be viewed and accessed from all pages in the publication. When you've decided where you want an object from the scratch area to be used, move it to its new location using any copying/pasting techniques.

FIGURE F-4: **Delete page warning box**

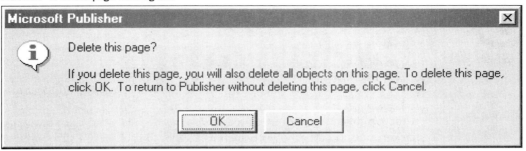

FIGURE F-5: **New last page of publication**

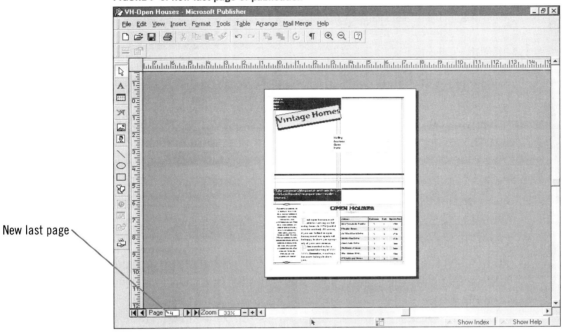

New last page

FIGURE F-6: **Two-page spread**

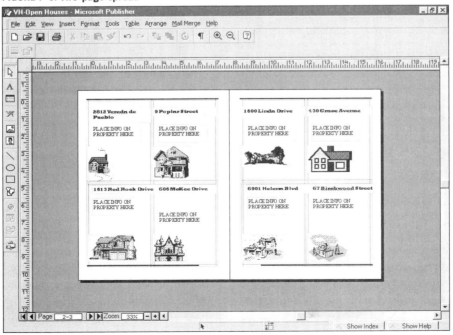

Working with a Background

Every publication has a page background that can be used to add text or objects that you want to be seen on every page. A publication without mirrored guides has a single background page, while a publication with mirrored guides has both left and right backgrounds. You can use the background to add an object, such as a logo, to each page or to only one page. ✏️ Lisa wants the listing in the bottom-right corner of the left-hand page to always display an exclusive listing. She adds the Vintage Homes logo (indicating an exclusive Vintage Homes listing) to the left background page of her publication to attract customers to the exclusive listings. She begins by switching to the background view.

1. Click **View** on the menu bar, then click **Go to Background**
   The background view displays, as shown in Figure F-7. Since you are adding an object to the left background page, you change to the single-page view.

2. Click **View** on the menu bar, click **Two-Page Spread** to deselect it, then click the **Left Background Page button** [🖥   ] on the horizontal scroll bar
   The left background page displays. You create a picture frame for the logo.

3. Click the **Picture Frame Tool** 🖼 on the Objects toolbar, drag the ✛ pointer from 5½" V/4½" H to 6¼" V/6½" H
   With the picture frame in place on the left background page, you insert the Vh-logo file on your Project Disk into the picture frame.

4. Right-click the **picture frame**, point to **Change Picture**, point to **Picture**, click **From File**, notice that the Insert Picture File dialog box opens, locate and click **Vh-logo**, then click **OK**
   The picture is inserted into the picture frame. You switch to foreground view and look at the last page of the publication to make sure the logo fits.

5. Click **View** on the menu bar, then click **Go to Foreground**
   The logo displays in the bottom-right quadrant of the page, as seen in Figure F-8. Now you display page 4 to verify that the left background image displays on the last page.

6. Click the **Last Page button** ▶️ on the horizontal scroll bar
   Compare your page to Figure F-9. The image is on the left background page and serves two purposes: to indicate exclusive Vintage Homes listings and to display the company's logo. Now you save your work.

7. Click the **Save button** 💾 on the Standard toolbar

Changing from double to single background pages

If you have mirrored layout guides, you also have left and right background pages. You can easily change from double to single background pages by deselecting the Create Two Backgrounds with Mirrored Guides check box in the Layout Guides dialog box. When this check box is not selected, you have only one background page. What was previously the right background page is now used as the publication's background page.

FIGURE F-7: **Left and right pages in background view**

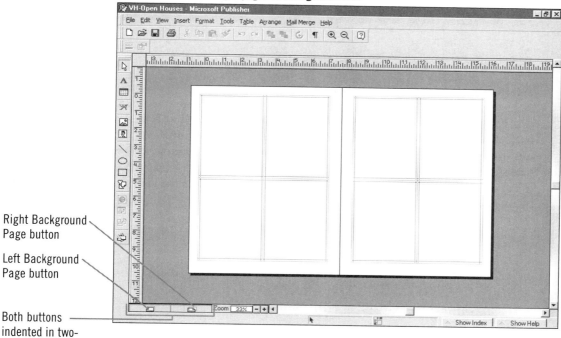

Right Background
Page button

Left Background
Page button

Both buttons
indented in two-
page spread

FIGURE F-8: **Image on page 2**

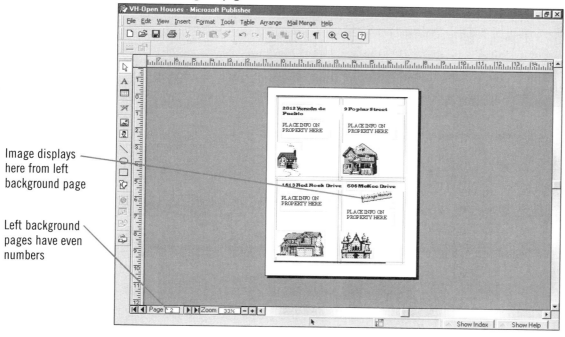

Image displays
here from left
background page

Left background
pages have even
numbers

FIGURE F-9: **Logo on left background page**

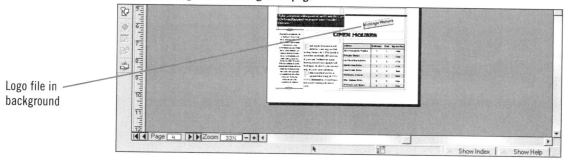

Logo file in
background

Creating a Header and Footer

Text that repeats on the top of each page is called a header, and text that repeats on the bottom of each page is a footer. In most cases, headers and footers are added to the background of pages. You have the option of ignoring the background on any page in the publication. You can create a text frame for the header or footer text and position it on the right or left background pages. Images can also be included in headers or footers to enhance the publication. Lisa wants to add a header to pages 2, 3, and 4 that contains a descriptive name for this publication. She begins by changing from foreground to background view, and she changes the view to the two-page spread. Because Lisa will be working in background view, it doesn't matter which page currently displays.

1. Click View on the menu bar, click Go to Background, click View on the menu bar, then click Two-Page Spread

   You add a text frame at the top-right corner of the left background page. Once one text frame is completed, you can copy it to the right background page. Use the guidelines to define the frame.

2. Click the Text Frame Tool A on the Objects toolbar, then drag the ✛ pointer from ⅛" V/4⅛" H to ½" V/7" H (snapping to the closest blue horizontal guidelines)

   The new text frame is selected in the publication. You zoom in to the frame.

3. Press [F9]

   You change to a style you created earlier and type the header text.

4. Click the Style list arrow on the Formatting toolbar, click Header/Footer, then type Open House Descriptions

   Compare your page to Figure F-10. You decide to use the quick copy feature to duplicate this text frame and place it on the right background page.

QuickTip

You can use any copy/paste method to duplicate text for a header or footer.

5. Press and hold [Ctrl], press and hold [Shift], position the ▷ pointer over the left background page text frame, press the left mouse button, when the pointer changes to ▷⁺, drag the copy of the frame so the top-left edge of the copy is at ⅛" V/8½" H, release the left mouse button, release [Ctrl], then release [Shift]

   You might want to use the scroll bars to reposition the screen so that you can see the text frames in both left and right background pages. Compare your headers to Figure F-11. Next, you change to the foreground view so you can see the headers.

6. Click View on the menu bar, click Go to Foreground, then click the Previous Page button ◀ on the horizontal scroll bar

   The header displays on pages 2 and 3, as shown in Figure F-12. You don't want the header to display on page 1. You zoom out so you can see the whole page, go to the first page, and ignore its background. Currently, the header is behind the pull quote, but you want to ignore the header just in case you move the quote later.

7. Press [F9], then click the First Page button ◀| on the horizontal scroll bar

8. Click View on the menu bar, then click Ignore Background

9. Click the Save button 🖫 on the Standard toolbar

FIGURE F-10: **Text frame for left background page header**

Header/Footer style

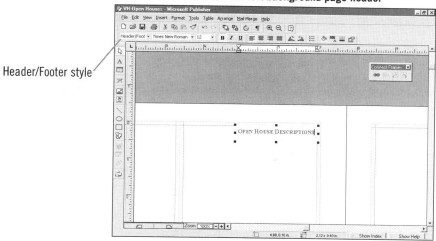

FIGURE F-11: **Headers on left and right background pages**

Right header

Left header

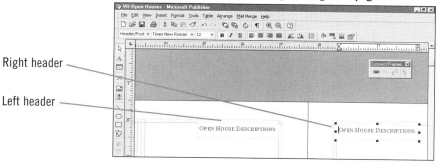

FIGURE F-12: **Headers visible on left and right facing pages**

Headers from
background pages

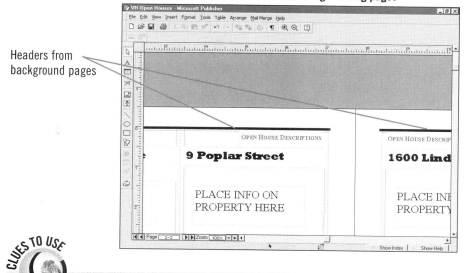

Masking background objects

Ignoring background elements is a good way to eliminate all background objects for a particular page. If, however, you want to ignore only some—but not all—background objects, using the Ignore Background command won't work. You can block out specific background elements by creating a mask in the foreground. Create a mask by clicking the Text Frame Tool A on the Objects toolbar and dragging the outline over the background element(s) you want to hide. Using this method, the background elements are preserved, and each page in a publication has exactly the look you want.

Publisher 98

Adding Page Numbers

You will probably want to add page numbers to publications that have more than two pages. Page numbers make it easy for readers to find stories that are continued on several pages. While you can manually insert page numbers within a text frame on a page, Publisher inserts the pound sign (#) where it will automatically place the calculated correct page number—in much the same way that it calculates page numbers for Continued on/Continued from notices. As pages are added and deleted, your page numbers will remain accurate. Like headers and footers, page numbers are added in background pages so they will appear on each page. ➤ Lisa wants page numbers to appear in a footer on every page, except page 1 (which already has its background ignored). She begins by changing to the background view.

1. **Click View on the menu bar, then click Go to Background**
   The background facing pages display. You want the page numbers to appear in the bottom-right corner of the left background page and the bottom-left corner of the right background page. You want to zoom in to the corners of the background pages.

2. **Press [F9], then position the screen using the scroll bars so the corners of the facing pages display, using Figure F-13 as a guide**
   You create a text frame on the left background page, although you could just as easily begin with the right background page.

3. **Click the Text Frame Tool A on the Objects toolbar, then drag the + pointer from 9⁹⁄₁₆" V/6½" H to 9¾" V/7" H**
   You want to use a style previously created for page numbers that displays a smaller font size.

4. **Click the Style list arrow on the Formatting toolbar, then click Page numbers**
   The font size changes to 8. You decide you want the word "Page" to appear before the actual page number.

5. **Type Page in the text frame, then press [Spacebar]**
   Page numbers are inserted using the menu bar.

6. **Click Insert on the menu bar, then click Page Numbers**
   The pound sign (#) appears in the text frame. When viewed in the foreground, the pound sign will automatically display the correct page number. Next, you quickly copy the text frame to the right background page.

7. **Press and hold [Ctrl], press and hold [Shift], position the pointer over the text frame, press the left mouse button, notice that the pointer changes to 🔖, drag the copy of the text frame so the left edge of the text frame is at 8½" H, release the left mouse button, release [Shift], then release [Ctrl]**
   Compare your work to Figure F-14. You return to the foreground view to see your work and display page 4.

8. **Click View on the menu bar, click Go to Foreground, then click the Last Page button ▶| on the horizontal scroll bar**
   Page 4 displays the page number at the bottom-right corner, as shown in Figure F-15. You zoom out, review page 1 to verify that the page number is not displayed, then save your work.

9. **Press [F9], click the First Page button |◀ on the horizontal scroll bar, then save your work**
   You can see that the page number does not display on page 1.

FIGURE F-13: **Background pages positioned on screen**

Location of footer text frames

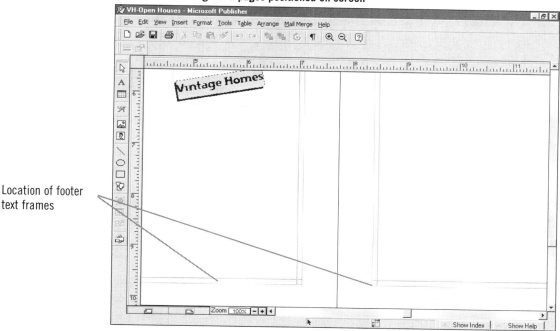

FIGURE F-14: **Text frame copied to right background page**

Pound sign (#) will display as the page number

Copied text frame

FIGURE F-15: **Results of page number footer**

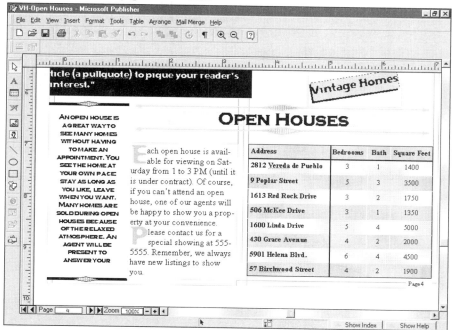

Publisher 98

Working with Stories

Text in a publication—called a story—can be typed directly into a text frame or prepared beforehand and inserted as a text file. In some cases, you might want to edit a story while working in Publisher. If a version of Microsoft Word 6.0 or later is installed on your computer, you can edit the story directly in Word. Editing directly in Word lets you take advantage of Word's features from within Publisher. After reading the publication, Lisa wants to modify an existing story on the first page.

1. **Click the text frame on the first page at 5" V/2" H, then press [F9]**
   The text frame is enlarged. You want to edit the story in this frame using Word.

Trouble?

If Word isn't installed on your computer, edit the story directly in Publisher. If you edit the story in Publisher, skip Step 5 and Step 7.

2. **Right-click the text frame, point to Change Text, click Edit Story in Microsoft Word, then click the Maximize button in the upper-right corner of the document window, so the document fills the window**
   Microsoft Word opens, displaying the story's text, as shown in Figure F-16. You want to change the word "What's" to "When's" and then delete text at the end of the first paragraph. Any edits you make to this text in Word will be applied to the text in the text frame in Publisher.

3. **Click to the right of the h in What's, press [Delete] twice, then type en**

Trouble?

Some text formatting, such as drop caps, is lost when moving from Word to Publisher.

4. **Select the text , so you want to take the time and make a good selection, then press [Delete]**
   You are ready to exit Word and return to the publication in Publisher.

5. **Click File on the menu bar, then click Exit**
   Word closes and you see that the selected text was deleted. You highlight the entire story so you can reformat the text.

6. **Right-click the text frame, point to Change Text, then select Highlight Entire Story**
   You want to add the drop caps that were deleted.

7. **Click Format on the menu bar, click Drop Cap, click the choice directly under the current selection, then click OK**
   The drop caps are inserted. Next, you make the text frame smaller so that it is closer in size to the image in the next column.

8. **Place the ⌖ pointer over the bottom-center handle, drag the ⌖ pointer to 6¾" V, then click outside the frame**
   Compare your text frame to Figure F-17. You decide to zoom out and save your work.

9. **Press [F9], then click the Save button 🖫 on the Standard toolbar**

FIGURE F-16: **Editing a story in Word**

Text to be deleted

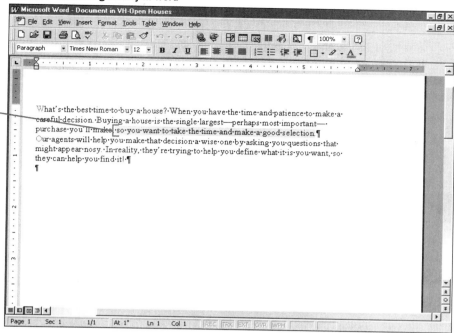

FIGURE F-17: **Edited story**

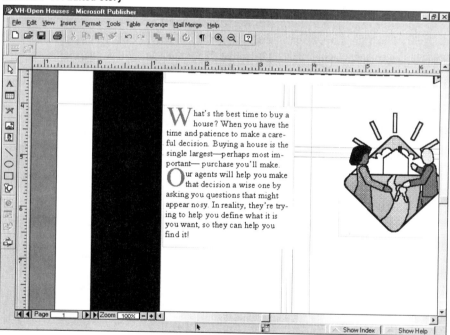

Copyfitting text

As you create a publication—particularly a newsletter—you may find that you have either too much or too little text. **Copyfitting** is a term used to describe the process of making the copy fit the space within a publication. If you have too much text, you can make the margins narrower, decrease the point size of the font, increase the

text frame, flow text into a frame on another page, or delete some text through editing. Solve the problem of too little text by inserting a graphic image or pull quote, making margins wider, increasing the point size of the font, or adding text. Once a text frame is selected, it can be copyfitted using the right mouse button.

Publisher 98

Using Tabs

A **tab**, or tab stop, is a defined location to which the insertion point advances when you press [Tab]. A table of contents uses tabs to align columnar information and lets readers locate the page numbers of specific stories within a publication. You make a table of contents by typing text into a text frame, and then adding tabs and dot leaders to connect the text and page number. **Dot leaders** are a series of dots that lead up to a tab. ✐ Lisa wants to add a table of contents so that readers can find information on specific properties easily. She'll use tabs to create the table of contents in a text frame at the bottom of page 1.

1. **Click the Text Frame Tool** [A] **on the Objects toolbar, drag the** + **pointer from 7" V/1¼" H to 9½" V/6½" H, then press [F9]**
   You change to the previously created style and type the title in the first line of the text frame.

2. **Click the Style list arrow on the Formatting toolbar, click Table of Contents, then type Table of Contents**
   You set a tab by double-clicking the location on the horizontal ruler. Double-clicking the horizontal ruler opens the Tabs dialog box.

QuickTip
You can also click Format on the menu bar, then click Tabs to open the Tabs dialog box.

3. **Double-click 4½" on the horizontal ruler**
   The Tabs dialog box opens, as shown in Figure F-18. You want the tab to have right alignment with a dot leader. **Right alignment** means that whatever you type at the tab will justify along the right edge at the tab stop.

4. **Click the Right Alignment option button, click the Dot Leader option button, then click OK**
   Now you advance to the tab to type the heading for the first line.

5. **Press [Tab]**
   A series of dots fills the space to the location of the insertion point.

6. **Type Page, then press [Enter]**
   The word Page is right-aligned at the tab stop. Next, you type the address of the first property and its page number.

7. **Type 2812 Vereda de Pueblo, press [Tab], type 2, then press [Enter]**
   Now you type in the information for the remaining properties.

8. **Type the remaining information, using Figure F-19 as a guide**
   You zoom out, save your work, and print the publication with your modifications. You review the publication and determine that it is complete for now.

9. **Press [F9], spell check your publication, click the Save button** [💾] **on the Standard toolbar, click the Print button** [🖨], **then close the publication**
   You are finished with this publication.

FIGURE F-18: Tabs dialog box

Defined tabs appear here

Alignment options

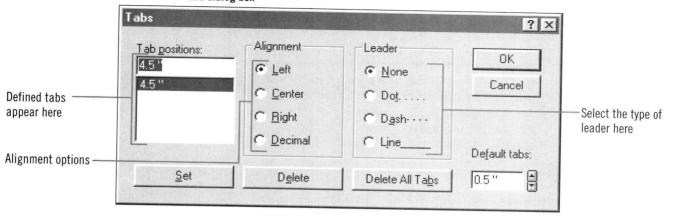

Select the type of leader here

FIGURE F-19: Completed table of contents

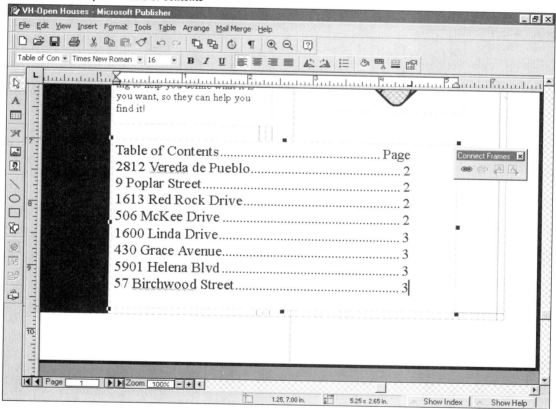

Creating a Booklet

Publisher refers to any publication that contains a series of folds (or binds) as a **booklet**. A booklet can be as small as a CD jewel-case label or it can contain 40 or 50 pages. Publisher contains many wizards that help you create a booklet. The advantage to using the Catalog to create a booklet is that the layout has been arranged in consideration of the necessary folds. ▰▰▰ Lisa wants to create a booklet that will be a certificate for potential customers. She creates the booklet using the Catalog and plans to fill in the necessary information later.

1. Click File on the menu bar, click New, click Gift Certificates on the Publications by Wizard tab, click the Blocks Gift Certificate, then click Start Wizard
   You want to create a gift certificate. You enter the information you need in the template and delete all unnecessary information.

Trouble?

If templates have been used previously, information may appear and the order of the Finish button may be different.

2. Click Next at the Wizard introduction screen, click Parrot color scheme, click Next, click Next to accept the deafult print tiling, click the Secondary option button, then click Finish
   You want to hide the wizard and modify the address.

3. Click the Hide Wizard button, right-click the text frame at ½" V/3" H, click Delete Object, create a text frame at 2½" V/3" H, then replace the existing text using Figure F-20 as a guide
   Now, you save the booklet as VH-Certificate on your Project Disk.

4. Click the Save button 🖫 on the Standard toolbar, type VH-Certificate, then click Save
   Next, you delete the existing WordArt frame and replace it with a picture frame.

5. Right-click the frame at 2¾" V/1" H, click Delete Object, click the Picture Frame Tool 🖼 on the Objects toolbar, then drag the + pointer from 2¼" V/½" H to 3¼" V/2¼" H
   You insert the electronic file containing the logo into the picture frame.

6. Right-click the picture frame, point to Change Picture, point to Picture, then click From File
   The Insert Picture File dialog box opens. You select the Vh-logo file from your Project Disk.

7. Locate and select the file Vh-logo, then click OK
   The picture displays in the frame, as shown in Figure F-21. Next, you save your work and print the booklet.

8. Click 🖫, then click the Print button 🖨 on the Standard toolbar
   When finished, exit Publisher.

9. Click File on the menu bar, then exit Publisher

FIGURE F-20: **Booklet created using Catalog**

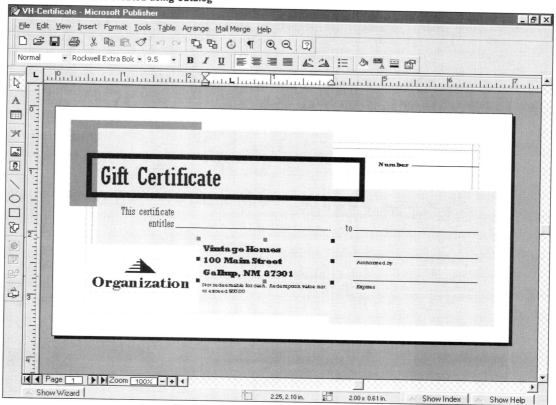

FIGURE F-21: **Logo inserted into picture frame**

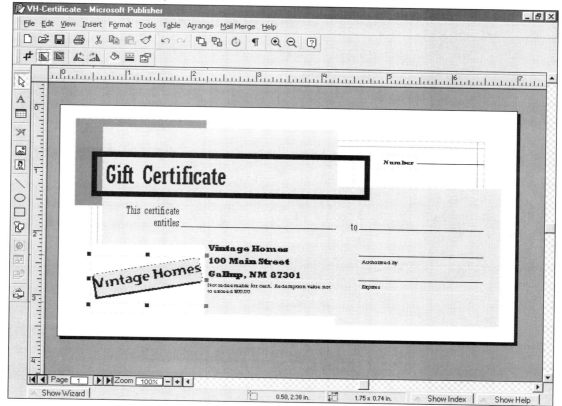

Practice

► Concepts Review

Label each of the elements of the Publisher window shown in **Figure F-22**.

FIGURE F-22

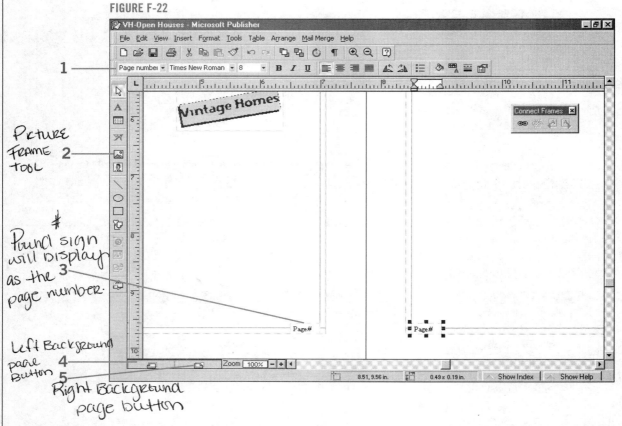

1 — Page number ▾ Times New Roman ▾ 8 ▾

PICTURE
FRAME 2 —
TOOL

Pound sign
will display
as the 3
page number.

Left Background
page 4 —
Button 5

Right Background
page button

Vintage Homes

Match each of the features with the buttons, menu, or command used to perform the function.

6. Changes between background and foreground D
7. Check to go to a specific page A
8. Text that repeats at the top of each page C
9. Deletes a page F
10. Adds dot leaders E
11. Changes styles B

a. Page ☐
b. Normal ▾
c. Header
d. View menu
e. Tabs dialog box
f. Edit menu

Select the best answer from the list of choices.

12. The gray area surrounding the page that can be used to save objects is called the:
a. Trash area.
b. Recycling area.
c. Scratch area.
d. Surplus area.

13. Each of the following is true about adding a page, *except*:
a. Pages can be added before or after the current page.
b. You can only add one page at a time.
c. Existing layout guides are added to the new page(s).
d. You can duplicate objects found on other pages in the publication.

14. Which button is used to change pages?
a. [AV icon]
b. [undo icon]
c. Page [   ]
d. Zoom [33%]

15. Which button is used to create a frame for a table of contents?
a. [table icon]
b. [picture icon]
c. A
d. [square icon]

16. Where in a publication are headers and footers usually placed?
a. Scratch area
b. Picture frame
c. In a central location
d. Background

17. Which menu is used to add page numbers to a publication?
a. Edit
b. Insert
c. Format
d. Tools

18. Text that appears at the bottom of every page is called a:
a. Header.
b. Style.
c. Repeater.
d. Footer.

19. Open the tabs dialog box by:
a. Using a command on the Edit menu.
b. Double-clicking a location on the horizontal ruler.
c. Double-clicking a location on the vertical ruler.
d. Using a command on the Table menu.

20. Which character creates automatic page numbers?
a. @
b. #
c. !
d. &

▶ Skills Review

If you complete all of the exercises in this unit, you may run out of space on your Project Disk. To make sure you have enough disk space, please copy files PUB F-2 through PUB F-5 to a new blank formatted disk. Use the new disk to complete the rest of the exercises in this unit. Throughout these exercises, use the zoom feature where necessary.

1. **Add a page.**
   a. Start Publisher.
   b. Open the file PUB F-2 and save it on your Project Disk as Whatsamatta News.
   c. Display page 2 in foreground view using the two-page spread view.
   d. Add two blank pages before page 2.
   e. Save your work.

2. **Delete a page.**
   a. Display page 2.
   b. Delete the newly added blank pages 2 and 3.
   c. Save your work.

3. **Work with a background.**
   a. Change to background view.
   b. Create a text frame from ½" V/5¾" H to ¾" V/8" H on page 2.
   c. Type "Read the Whatsamatta News Bulletin."
   d. Save your work.

4. **Create a header and footer.**
   a. Draw a text frame from 10" V/½" H to 10¼" V/3" H on the left background page.
   b. Type "Great students read Whatsamatta News."
   c. Copy this text frame so that its bottom-left edge is at 10¼" V/14" H on the right background page.
   d. Save the publication.

5. **Add page numbers.**
   a. Create a text frame from 10" V/9" H to 10¼" V/9½" H on the right background page.
   b. Type "Page", then press [Spacebar].
   c. Insert page numbers.
   d. Copy this text frame to the left background page so that its bottom-right edge is at 10¼" V/8" H.
   e. Return to foreground view.
   f. Save the publication.

6. **Work with stories.**
   a. Display page 2.
   b. Select the story at 2" V/2" H.
   c. Open Word to edit the story.
   d. Add the following text at the end of the story: "This new lab has state-of-the-art equipment, including Pentium MMX computers with oodles of memory, zip drives for student storage, 6 flat-bed scanners, and 6 color laser printers, and all stations have 17" monitors. Just can't wait to take those desktop publishing courses!"
   e. Exit Word.
   f. Verify that the text has been added to the story.
   g. Save the publication.

7. **Use tabs.**
   a. Display page 1.
   b. Create a text frame from 8½" V/2½" H to 10⅛" V/7¾" H.
   c. Create a right-aligned tab stop with dot leaders at 3½" inches in the first line of the table of contents.
   d. Change the current font size to 12 points.
   e. Using the default style, type "Topic" as the title of the first column, then type "Page" as the title of the second column.
   f. Enter page numbers for the following newsletter headings: "More Computer Courses", "New Computer Lab Completed", "English Department Expanded", "Great Concerts Scheduled", "Recycling Begins On Campus", and "Campus Pool Hours Expanded".
   g. Save and print your work. Placeholders can be modified at a later date.
   h. Close the publication.

8. **Create a booklet.**
   a Use the Catalog to create a menu for Cool Guy's Cantina.
   b. Save the menu as Cool Guy's Cantina on your Project Disk.
   c. Personalize the text by adding the following: "managed by *type your name.*"
   d. Change any other text as you see fit.
   e. Save your work.
   f. Print the publication.
   g. Read and follow the folding instructions.
   h. Exit Publisher.

▶ Independent Challenges

1. You recently volunteered with your local Humane Society. You love taking care of the animals, but you've also volunteered to write the organization's newsletter. Use your Publisher skills to make this a professional-looking publication.
   To complete this independent challenge:

   a. Start Publisher, and open the file PUB F-3. Update the embedded objects, initialize the printer, then save it as Humane Society News on your Project Disk.
   b. Add at least one page to this publication.
   c. Add page numbers in a footer. (Move any information so that your header/footer fits correctly.)
   d. Add a title in a header or footer.
   e. Make sure the page number—or header/footer—does not appear on the first page.
   f. Make up your own headings to replace the existing placeholders.
   g. Create a table of contents on the first page of the newsletter.
   h. Use dot leaders in the table of contents.
   i. Save the publication.
   j. Spell check the publication.
   k. Print the publication.
   l. Exit Publisher.

2. A local elementary school has hired you to produce a newsletter as a morale booster for its staff. You've begun working on the project and need to complete it.
   To complete this independent challenge:

   a. Start Publisher, open the file PUB F-4, and save it as Eliot Elementary School on your Project Disk.
   b. Add page numbers and a header or footer. (Move any information so that your header/footer fits correctly.)
   c. Make sure the page number—or header/footer—does not appear on the first page.
   d. Make up your own headings to replace the existing placeholders.
   e. Replace at least one story with your own original story.
   f. Edit the story in Word if you have this program available to you; otherwise, edit in Publisher.
   g. Spell check the publication.
   h. Create a table of contents on the first page of the newsletter.
   i. Use dot leaders in the table of contents.
   j. Save the publication.
   k. Print the publication.
   l. Exit Publisher.

3. You've decided to organize and improve your collection of CDs. Start with a jewel case—and its liner—that were ruined when a mysterious substance spilled on it at a recent party. You have already bought a replacement jewel case; now you will create its liner.

To complete this independent challenge:

a. Start Publisher if necessary.

b. Use the Catalog to create a label for a CD.

c. Save the publication on your Project Disk as CD Liner.

d. Add text for your favorite CD, adding any artwork or drawn objects.

e. Edit the text in Word if you have this program available to you; otherwise, edit in Publisher.

f. Arrange the information in an attractive format, using your graphics skills.

g. Save and print the publication.

4. Your research on television stations has led you to the World Wide Web. As a member of the Media and Communications Information League, you have been assigned the duty of preparing a short newsletter listing television Web sites that will be distributed to its membership.

To complete this independent challenge:

a. Log on to the Internet and use your browser to go to http://www.course.com. From there, click the link Student Online Companions, click Microsoft Publisher 98—Introductory, then click the link for Unit F.

b. Use each of the sites to obtain Web addresses that you can include in your newsletter.

c. Additionally, find other Web sites for television stations.

d. Use the Catalog to create a newsletter called TV News Galore.

e. Save the file as News Galore on your Project Disk.

f. Create a text frame that lists your Web addresses.

g. Add page numbers to the newsletter if necessary.

h. Create a header or footer or modify the existing ones.

i. Replace heading placeholders with your own headings.

j. Create a table of contents on the first page for those headings.

k. Save the publication.

l. Print the publication.

► Visual Workshop

Open the file PUB F-5 and save it on your Project Disk as EMS promo. Use Word to modify the text in the frame on the right side of the publication (at 4" V/6" H) so it looks like Figure F-23. Save and print the publication.

FIGURE F-23

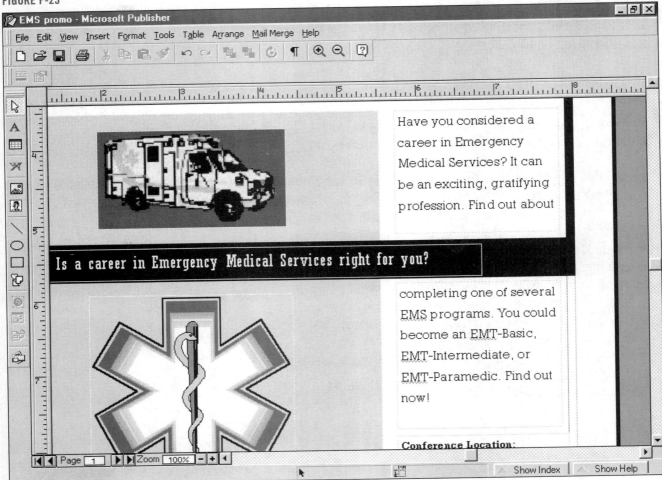

Using
Special Features

Objectives

- ► Add BorderArt
- ► Create an object shadow
- ► Design WordArt
- ► Create a bleed
- ► Create a watermark
- ► Wrap text around a frame
- ► Rotate a text frame
- ► Create a Web page

Now that you know how to use Publisher to create a publication, you're ready to explore the special features that add interesting elements to your work and add effects found in professionally created publications. Publisher's special features, which are fun and easy to use, will enable you to add fancy borders to frames, use the scratch area to work with objects, design curved text, wrap text around a frame, rotate text frames, and create Web pages. ◄━━ Rachel Kennedy is the account executive for the EMT Academy, a private school specializing in training Emergency Medical Technicians. Rachel is putting the finishing touches on a new recruiting brochure.

Adding BorderArt

Attractive borders can add pizzazz to a publication. Borders can be added to any frame. As with any design elements, judicious use creates a professional look. Rather than having to spend a lot of time creating these borders, users can take advantage of **BorderArt**, which contains more than 160 decorative borders. BorderArt is added to a frame using a tab in the BorderArt dialog box. ◄— Rachel wants to add a simple border design to the first page of the brochure. She enlarges the area at the top of the first page.

1. Before you start this unit, copy the file **PUB G-1** from your Project Disk to a new blank formatted disk

2. Start **Publisher**, open the file **PUB G-1**, click **OK** to initialize your printer, click **Yes** to update all embedded objects if necessary, then save the file as **EMT brochure**
   You will make use of the **scratch area**, the gray work area surrounding the displayed publication page(s), to work with an object. Several graphic images are on the scratch area that you will use later. First, you select the gray oval on page 1.

3. Click the **gray oval** at 1" V/2" H, press **[F9]**, then scroll using the vertical scroll bar if necessary to make sure you can see the upper edge of the blue rectangle
   You select the blue box behind the oval—a rectangle sent behind the other objects on the page—before adding the BorderArt.

4. Click the **blue rectangle** at 1" V/½" H
   Compare your screen to Figure G-1.

QuickTip
You can also open the Border Style dialog box by clicking Format on the menu bar, pointing to Line/Border Style, then clicking More Styles.

5. Right-click the **blue rectangle**, point to **Change Rectangle**, point to **Line/Border Style**, then click **More Styles**
   The Border Style dialog box opens. You choose a simple border that won't detract from the existing design.

6. Click the **BorderArt tab**, scroll through the list of Available Borders, then click **Basic...White Squares**
   Figure G-2 shows the BorderArt tab with the Basic White Squares border selected. Available borders are listed in alphabetical order and sample patterns are shown. When you click a border, the sample displays around the perimeter of the Preview box.

QuickTip
Remove existing BorderArt from a frame by opening the Border Style dialog box, selecting None, the first option in the list of Available Borders, then clicking OK.

7. Click **OK**
   The BorderArt pattern appears on the edge of the background, as shown in Figure G-3. Now that the BorderArt is added to the object, you zoom out and save your work.

8. Press **[F9]**, then click the **Save button** 🖫 on the Standard toolbar

FIGURE G-1: **Object selected**

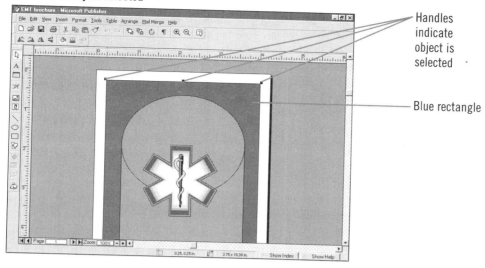

Handles indicate object is selected

Blue rectangle

FIGURE G-2: **Border Style dialog box**

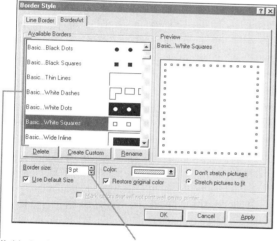

FIGURE G-3: **BorderArt added to object**

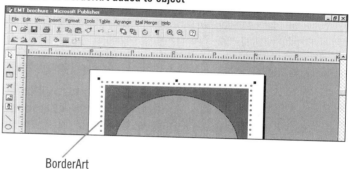

BorderArt

Available borders appear here

Click to change the size of the border

Create custom BorderArt

Almost any simple clip art or graphic image can be turned into BorderArt. Once the BorderArt tab in the Border Style dialog box is selected, click Create Custom. You can choose from images in the Clip Gallery or elsewhere on your computer. Click the Choose Picture button, locate the image, click OK, choose a name for your border, then click OK. Figure G-4 shows a custom border created from the Clip Gallery.

FIGURE G-4: **Custom border in Border Style dialog box**

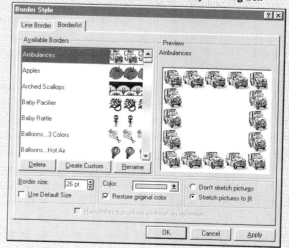

Creating an Object Shadow

There are many ways to call attention to text on a page besides using fonts, font sizes, and character formats. For example, you can add or delete an object shadow using a button on the Formatting toolbar. Shadows add the illusion of depth. When applied, an object shadow appears behind the currently selected frame. Rachel wants to add a shadow behind the text frame on page 4 so it looks like it is lifting off the page in a 3-D effect. She displays page 4, selects the text frame, and zooms in.

Steps 1 2 3 4

1. **Click the Last Page button** ▶ **on the horizontal scroll bar, click the text frame at 10" V/2" H, then press [F9]**
   The text frame is enlarged. You use the Shadow command to add the shadow.

2. **Click Format on the menu bar, then click Shadow**
   The shadow appears behind the text in the frame, as shown in Figure G-5. Now you want to change the fill color inside the text frame to make it look more dramatic.

3. **Click Format on the menu bar, point to Fill Color, then click More Colors**
   The Colors dialog box opens, as shown in Figure G-6. You choose the color gray to compliment the gray shadow color.

4. **Click the Gray-25% color box in column 10 in the Black row, then click OK**
   The gray color is applied to fill the text frame, as shown in Figure G-7. You zoom out and save your work.

5. **Press [F9], then click the Save button** 🖫 **on the Standard toolbar**

QuickTip

You can see how a color looks before closing the Colors dialog box by clicking Apply. You may have to relocate the dialog box so you can see the applied color.

FIGURE G-5: Enlarged text frame with shadow

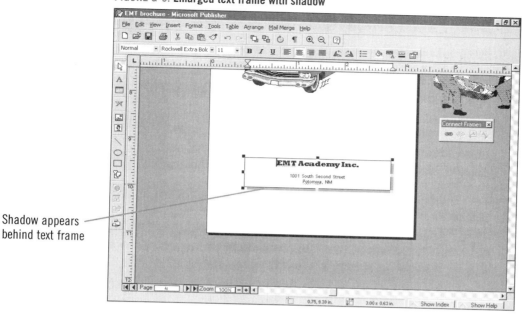

Shadow appears
behind text frame

FIGURE G-6: Colors dialog box

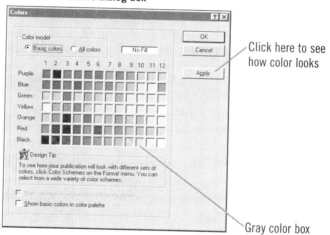

Click here to see
how color looks

Gray color box

FIGURE G-7: New color applied to text frame

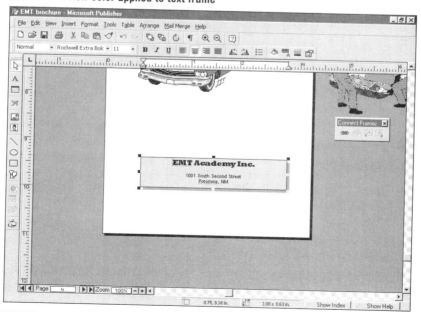

Designing WordArt

You have probably seen text in documents and publications that is designed to fill a shape that may be curved or wavy. You can easily create this effect using WordArt. This program, which is automatically started from within Publisher, gives you a wide variety of text styles and effects from which to choose. Text can be transformed into many shapes, shadows and patterns can be added, and text color can be changed. ◀— Rachel wants to add WordArt to the oval at the top of page 1 to identify the academy's name. She displays page 1, selects the oval, and zooms in.

Steps 1 2 3 4

1. **Click the First Page button** 🔳 **on the horizontal scroll bar, click the oval object at 1" V/2" H, then press [F9]**
   The oval object on page 1 is enlarged. You create the text effect by clicking the WordArt button on the Objects toolbar, then drawing a frame for the design.

2. **Click the WordArt Frame Tool** 🖈 **on the Objects toolbar, then drag the + pointer from ⅝" V/¾" H to 2⅛" V/3⅝" H**
   The WordArt window opens, as shown in Figure G-8. The text typed in the Enter Your Text Here text box is displayed in the newly drawn frame.

3. **Type EMT Academy in the Enter Your Text Here text box, then click Update Display**
   The display now contains the new text. You want to change the font to make the text look more dramatic. Table G-1 shows commonly used WordArt toolbar buttons.

4. **Click the Font list arrow** `Arial ▾` **on the WordArt toolbar, then click Felix Titling**
   The text "EMT Academy" now displays in the new font. Next you change the shape of the WordArt so the text curves to fill the shape.

5. **Click the Shape list arrow** `— Plain Text ▾` **on the WordArt toolbar, then click the first WordArt shape in the third row**
   The shape you chose is called Arch Up (Pour). You decide to add a shadow to the characters. A WordArt shadow adds dimension to the characters within the WordArt object.

6. **Click the Shadow button** 🔲 **on the WordArt toolbar**
   The Shadow dialog box opens, as shown in Figure G-9.

7. **Click the third shadow from the left, then click OK**
   The dialog box closes and the shadow is seen in the design. You close WordArt and return to the publication.

8. **Click anywhere on the scratch area**
   Compare your page to Figure G-10. Now you zoom out and save your work.

9. **Press [F9], then click the Save button** 🔲 **on the Standard toolbar**

FIGURE G-8: WordArt window

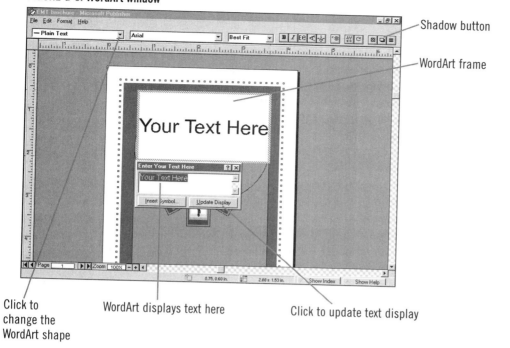

Shadow button

WordArt frame

Click to change the WordArt shape

WordArt displays text here

Click to update text display

FIGURE G-9: Shadow dialog box in WordArt

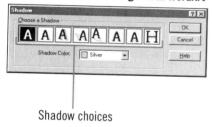

Shadow choices

FIGURE G-10: WordArt design in publication

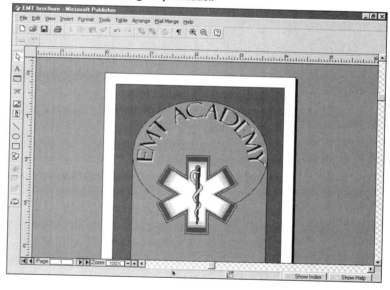

TABLE G-1: Commonly used WordArt toolbar buttons

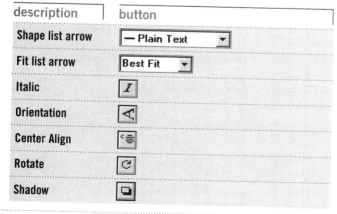

description	button		description	button
Shape list arrow	— Plain Text ▼		Font list arrow	Arial ▼
Fit list arrow	Best Fit ▼		Bold	**B**
Italic	*I*		Upper/Lower case	Ee
Orientation	◁		Stretch	⌅
Center Align	≣		Character Spacing	AV
Rotate	↻		Color/Pattern	▨
Shadow	▢		Line width	≡

Creating a Bleed

Bleeds are used to make objects run off the edge of a page, such as section indicators in a book. Because a laser printer uses the edges of the paper to pull the paper within it, however, it is not possible to print all the way to the edge of a page. When the page is printed, the object prints as much as the printer is capable of printing. If you want an object to run off the edge of a page, you have to trim the page after it has been printed. Rachel wants to create a decorative shape on the top of the last page of the publication. This shape will extend beyond the edge of the right edge of the last page (onto the scratch area). After she creates the shape, she will rotate it to make it look more dramatic.

Steps 1 2 3 4

Trouble?

You may need to change the size of the publication.

1. Click the Last Page button ▶| on the horizontal scroll bar
Page 4 displays, as seen in Figure G-11. Now, you create a box along the top of the page. It does not matter how much the box extends into the scratch area, as long as it extends beyond the page.

2. Click the Rectangle Tool ▢ on the Objects toolbar, then drag the + pointer from 1" V/0" H to 2" V/5" H
A solid black box displays, as shown in Figure G-12. You decide to zoom in to the box.

QuickTip

If an object extends beyond the left edge of a page, the initial horizontal coordinate is a negative number.

3. Press [F9]
The box is enlarged. Now you rotate the box 10 degrees to make it look more attractive.

4. Click the Rotate button ↻ on the Formatting toolbar
The Custom Rotate dialog box opens, as shown in Figure G-13. Now you rotate the box 10 degrees.

5. Click the Counterclockwise button twice, then click Close
The box is rotated 10 degrees. You zoom out to examine the page.

6. Press [F9]
Compare your page to Figure G-14. Now you save your work.

7. Click the Save button 🖫 on the Standard toolbar

FIGURE G-11: **Preparing to create a bleed**

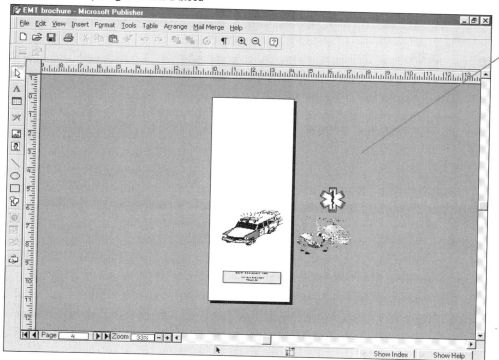

Box will extend onto scratch area

FIGURE G-12: **Rectangle will bleed to page edge**

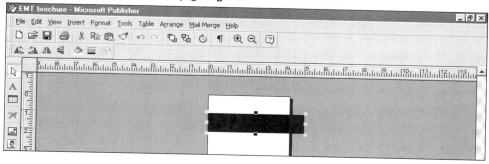

FIGURE G-13: **Custom Rotate dialog box**

Click to rotate counterclockwise

Click to eliminate any rotation

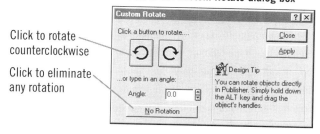

FIGURE G-14: **Rotate object for bleed**

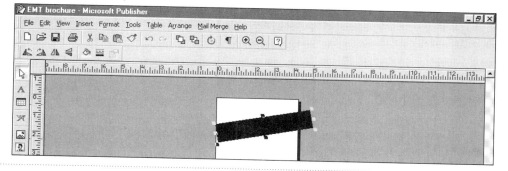

Creating a Watermark

You have probably seen an image or text in the background of high-quality paper stock. This effect is known as a watermark. A **watermark** is a lightly shaded image that appears behind other objects on a page. It is an effective way of making a statement or identifying a product, mission, or institution in a subtle manner. In some situations, such as a multipage newsletter or poster, you may want to add a watermark to a publication's background page(s). Rachel decides to place an emergency medical symbol—the Star of Life—as a watermark, but only on the last page. If she wanted the watermark to appear on every page, she would add it to the background. The image, already available on the scratch area, needs to be resized and then recolored.

Steps 1 2 3 4

1. **Click the Star of Life image in the scratch area**
   The image is selected, as shown in Figure G-15. You want to resize the image—while maintaining its original scale—so that it fills the last page.

2. **Position the pointer over the top-right handle, press and hold [Shift], drag the ⌐ pointer to 1½" V/10" H, release the mouse button, then release [Shift]**
   The image is resized. Now you are ready to move the image to the page.

3. **Position the pointer over the image, then drag the pointer so that the top-left edge of the image is at 3¾" V/0" H**
   Compare your screen to Figure G-16. The Star of Life image automatically appears behind the ambulance.

4. **Right-click the Star of Life image, point to Change Picture, then click Recolor Picture**
   The Recolor Picture dialog box opens. You choose the gray color so that the image will appear faintly and match the text fill color on the page.

5. **Click the Color list arrow, click the Gray-25% color box in Recent Colors, then click OK**
   The image changes to the gray color and appears faintly in the background as a watermark, as shown in Figure G-17. Now, you save your work.

6. **Click the Save button 💾 on the Standard toolbar**

FIGURE G-15: **Selected Star of Life for watermark**

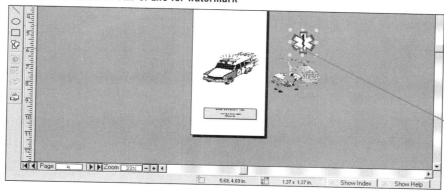

Image will be
resized and
recolored

FIGURE G-16: **Image resized and moved onto page**

Selected image
automatically
moved behind
other image

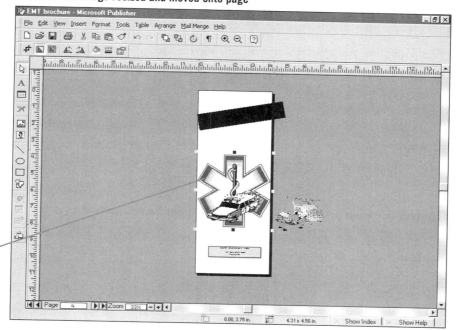

FIGURE G-17: **Completed watermark image**

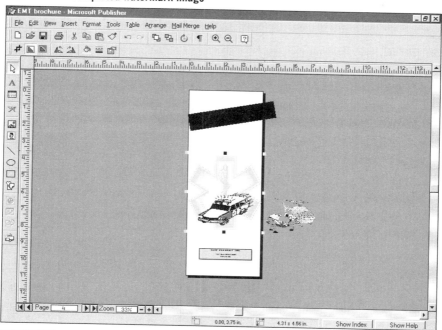

Wrapping Text Around a Frame

A story can be made to look elegant by wrapping the text around the frame of images in the story. Depending on the width of an image, a story will appear at the top and bottom or along the sides of an image inserted into a text frame. For added effect, you can make the text flow more closely to the outlines of the graphic image. Two buttons on the Formatting toolbar control text wrap. The Wrap Text to Frame button causes text to wrap around the perimeter of a picture's frame— usually a rectangle. The Wrap Text to Picture button on the Formatting toolbar causes text to wrap around the picture—usually an irregular shape. Rachel has an image of EMTs she wants to insert in a text frame on page 3. She wants to see how the text looks if it wraps around the image. She changes pages, selects the story, and zooms in.

1. Click the Previous Page button ◀ on the horizontal scroll bar, click the text frame at 4" V/6" H, then click the Zoom In button ➕ on the horizontal scroll bar three times
   The zoom percentage you use will vary with your monitor. You want to read the text and see the image on the scratch area. Once the story and image are visible, you select the image and move it into the story.

2. Click the EMT image on the scratch area, then drag the 🚑 pointer so that the top-left edge of the image is at 5" V/4¾" H
   The image disappears behind the text. Next you bring the image to the front, then decide to wrap the text to the picture.

QuickTip

In a story with hyphenation, you may turn this feature off by clicking Tools, pointing to Language, clicking Hyphenate, then clicking OK to keep words from splitting around an image.

3. Click the Bring to Front button 🗗 on the Standard toolbar, then click the Wrap Text to Picture button 🖼 on the Formatting toolbar
   See Figure G-18. The text now conforms more closely to the image. You think the image is too large, though, and would like to change the size of the image in the story. You resize the image to make it smaller so that it doesn't overwhelm the text.

4. Press and hold [Shift], position the pointer on the upper-right corner of the image, drag the 🔲 pointer so that the top-right edge of the image is at 7" H, release the mouse button, then release [Shift]
   You move the image up to reposition it in the story.

Trouble?

Text wrapping may differ slightly depending on the location and size of the image.

5. Position the pointer on the image, when it changes to 🚑, drag the image so that the top-left edge is at 4" V
   Now, you make the text frame longer so that the hidden text displays.

6. Click the text frame, position the pointer over the center-bottom handle, then drag the 🔲 pointer to 8½" V
   The entire story is displayed, as seen in Figure G-19. You zoom out.

7. Click the Zoom Out button ➖ on the horizontal scroll bar until the entire page displays on the screen at a 33% zoom level
   You like the way the image looks and decide to save your work.

8. Click the Save button 💾 on the Standard toolbar

FIGURE G-18: Graphic image inserted in text frame

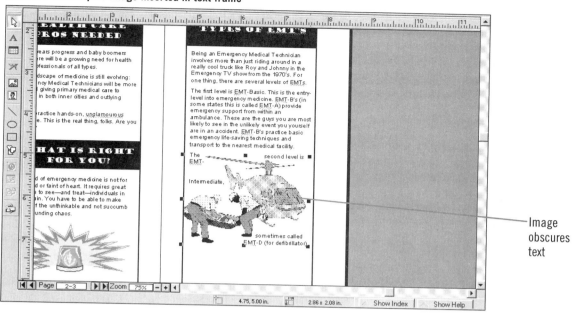

Image obscures text

FIGURE G-19: Text wrapped to frame

Image resized and moved

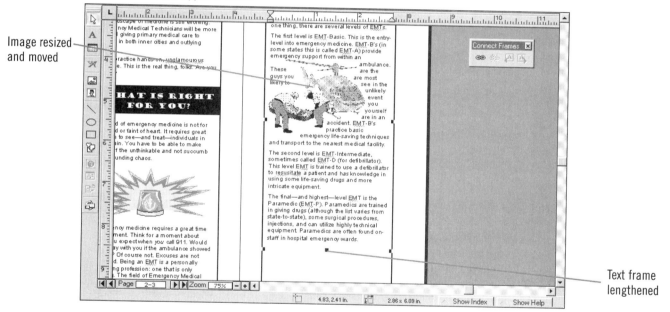

Text frame lengthened

CLUES TO USE

Editing an irregular shape

Not all figures have perfectly rectangular shapes. Because of these irregular shapes, Publisher lets you display and edit the handles surrounding irregularly shaped frames. Click the Edit Irregular Wrap button ⬚ on the Formatting toolbar to display each of the handles in such a shape. Figure G-20 shows the handles on an irregularly shaped image. Click and drag any handle so that the text wraps with a more pleasing effect.

FIGURE G-20: Handles surrounding an irregularly shaped picture

Click to display handles

Drag individual handles to resize the frame

Rotating a Text Frame

WordArt is an effective way of creating special text effects, but you can rotate any text frame using the same techniques used to rotate a graphic image. This approach is an effective design technique used to call attention to text. Rachel wants to reinforce the message of the brochure by adding a rotated text frame on the last page. She'll create the text frame on the scratch area, then rotate it and move it into position on the left edge of the page. First, she displays the publication's last page.

Steps 1 2 3 4

1. **Click the Last Page button ▶ on the horizontal scroll bar**
   The last page of the publication displays. You use the text button to create a text frame on the scratch area.

2. **Click the Text Frame Tool A on the Objects toolbar, then drag the + pointer from 1" V/6" H to 1⅝" V/13" H**
   You select a previously created style for the contents of the text frame.

3. **Click the Style list arrow on the Formatting toolbar, then click EMT headline**
   Now you type the text in the frame. Because the font used in this style contains only capital letters, you do not need to press [CapsLock] or use [Shift] to type this text.

4. **Type BE AN EMT: SAVE LIVES**
   Compare your screen to Figure G-21. Now you rotate the text frame 90 degrees.

5. **Click the Rotate button ⟳ on the Standard toolbar, the Custom Rotate dialog box opens, type 90 in the Angle text box, then click Close**
   The text frame is rotated 90 degrees—in fact, some of the frame is not visible, as seen in Figure G-22. Next, you move the text frame into position on the page.

6. **Position the pointer on the selected frame, when it changes to 🚚 drag the text frame so that the top-left edge is at 0" V/¼" H**
   You want the background of the text frame to be clear so you can see the watermark and the rectangle that bleeds to the right edge. You change the object color of the frame to clear.

7. **Click the Fill Color button ◈ on the Formatting toolbar, then click No Fill**
   Compare your work to Figure G-23. There are a few spelling errors in this publication, so you check the spelling and correct any mistakes in all the stories.

8. **Press [F7], correct all spelling errors and ignore all correctly spelled proper nouns, then close the Spelling dialog box when you are done**
   You save your work and print pages 1 and 4 of the publication.

9. **Click the Save button 💾 on the Standard toolbar, click File on the menu bar, click Print, click the All 4 pages option button, then click OK**

FIGURE G-21: **Text in frame on scratch area**

Click to rotate frame

Selected style

Text frame will be
rotated 90 degrees

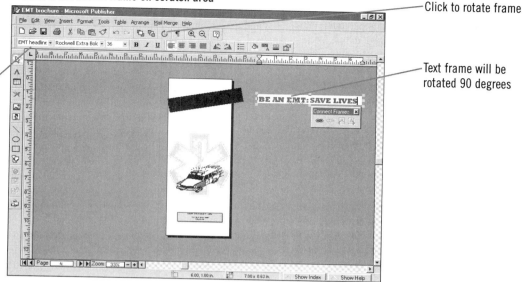

FIGURE G-22: **Rotated text frame on scratch area**

Part of text frame
is not visible

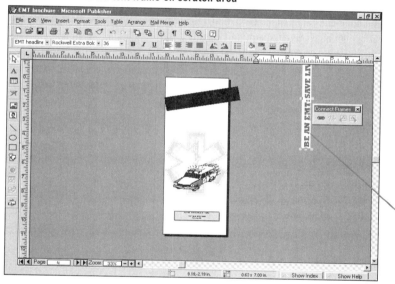

FIGURE G-23: **Completed rotated text frame**

Using No
Fill option
makes
bleed and
watermark
visible

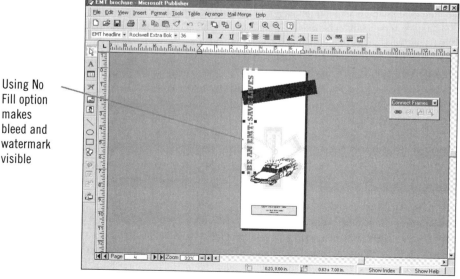

Creating a Web Page

You can create a Web page using the Catalog, or you can design a Web page from scratch. The Catalog uses design conventions specifically used on the Web. You can also use any existing publication and Publisher's conversion utility. The conversion utility automatically creates a duplicate file in a format acceptable for Web pages. Because elements used in print material don't always make for good Web pages, you can use the Design Checker to alert you to any design problems. ◢ Rachel anticipates that the EMT Academy might want to utilize this brochure on its Web site. She uses the conversion utility and Design Checker to see what additional work might need to be done. She can use that information to advise the client.

1. **Click File on the menu bar, then click Create Web Site from Current Publication**
   The publication remains on the screen, but the title bar now indicates that this is a new, untitled, unsaved publication. The Design Checker warning box opens, as shown in Figure G-24. You want to use the Design Checker to check all the pages in this publication.

QuickTip

Click Tools on the menu bar, then click Design Checker to start the Design Checker at any time.

2. **Click Yes in the Design Checker dialog box, make sure the All option button is selected, then click OK**
   The Design Checker begins, starting at page 1. The checker stops at the first problem it encounters and displays a dialog box with advice, as shown in Figure G-25. You read the dialog box then continue the Design Checker.

3. **Click Ignore All**
   The Design Checker continues to find more design problems. You determine you can advise your client that much work will be required to use this existing page on the Web. You close the Design Checker.

4. **Click Close**
   You are returned to the unnamed publication. You decide to preview the publication using your Web browser.

Trouble?

If you don't have a browser, skip to Step 7. If your browser automatically connects you to the Web, click Cancel in the Connect To dialog box.

5. **Click the Web Site Preview button 🔍 on the Standard toolbar**
   The Preview Web Site box displays the progress of Publisher as the Web site is created. Your default browser opens displaying the one-page Web site, as shown in Figure G-26. You decide to read the Web site, then close the browser.

6. **Scroll through the Web site document, then click the browser's Close button**
   You exit Publisher without saving the unsaved publication.

7. **Click File on the menu bar, click Exit Publisher, then click No when asked to save your changes**

Publishing to the Web

Once your publication is free of spelling errors and has been through the Design Checker, you're ready to publish your document on the Web. Web documents use a special format called HTML (HyperText Markup Language) and the next step is to convert your publication into HTML using Publisher menu commands. First you must click File on the menu bar, then click Create Web Site from Current Publication. If you have an active Internet connection and have the Web Publishing Wizard installed, you can click File on the menu bar, click Publish to Web, then follow the instructions to upload your document. If the Web Publishing Wizard is not installed, you can download it from the Microsoft Publisher Web site. You can also publish your document to another (offline) location by clicking File on the menu bar, then clicking Publish Web Site to Folder. Indicate where you want the document saved.

FIGURE G-24: **Design Checker warning box**

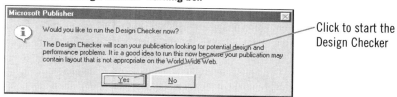

Click to start the
Design Checker

FIGURE G-25: **Design Checker in progress**

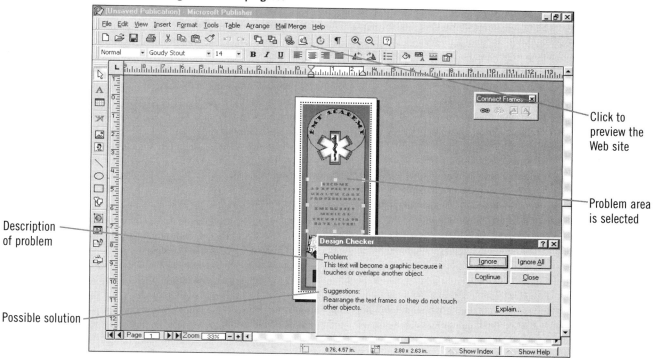

Click to
preview the
Web site

Problem area
is selected

Description
of problem

Possible solution

FIGURE G-26: **Previewed Web site in browser**

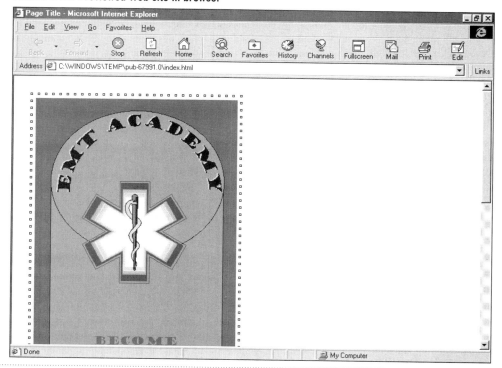

Practice

▶ Concepts Review

Label each of the elements of the Publisher window shown in Figure G-27.

FIGURE G-27

Match each of the buttons with the statement that describes its function.

7. Wraps text to frame E

8. Wraps text to picture C

9. Creates a rectangle B

10. Edits irregular shape F

11. Preview a Web site A

12. Creates WordArt D

a. 🔍

b. ☐

c. ▣

d. ✕

e. ▣

f. ▣

Select the best answer from the list of choices.

13. A watermark can be:
   a. Rotated.
   b. Recolored.
   c. Created in the background view.
   d. All of the above.

14. Each of the following is true about WordArt, *except*:
   a. The program is started from within Publisher.
   b. WordArt objects can be added only to the foreground view.
   c. WordArt can be resized like any other object.
   d. WordArt can be edited.

15. Which button is used to create WordArt?
   a.
   b.
   c.
   d.

16. If you click the Counterclockwise button twice, the box rotates:
   a. 10 degrees.
   b. 20 degrees.
   c. -10 degrees.
   d. -20 degrees.

17. The area surrounding a publication page is called the:
   a. Scrap area.
   b. Recycling area.
   c. Scratch area.
   d. Desktop area.

18. Which feature creates curved text?
   a. TextMaker
   b. WordWinder
   c. Design Checker
   d. WordArt

19. An object that extends beyond a page's border(s) is called a(n):
   a. Bleed.
   b. Bleeder.
   c. Edger.
   d. Flow.

20. A lightly shaded image appearing behind other images is called a:
   a. Waterbleed.
   b. Watersort.
   c. Watertype.
   d. Watermark.

21. Which button is used to wrap text to a picture?
   a.
   b.
   c.
   d.

► Skills Review

If you complete all of the exercises in this unit, you may run out of space on your Project Disk. To make sure you have enough disk space, please copy files PUB G-2 through PUB G-5 to a new disk. Use the new disk to complete the rest of the exercises in this unit.

Throughout these exercises, use the zoom feature where necessary.

1. **Add BorderArt.**
   a. Start Publisher.
   b. Open the file PUB G-2, initialize the printer, then save the file on your Project Disk as Aztec Film Society.
   c. Select the large frame in the flyer.
   d. Apply the Twisted Lines 2 BorderArt pattern to the rectangle using the default settings.
   e. Choose No Fill for the rectangle.
   f. Save your work.

2. **Create an object shadow.**
   a. Select the text frame at 7" V/3" H.
   b. Apply a shadow to the text frame.
   c. Save your work.

3. **Design WordArt.**
   a. Create a WordArt object from 2" V/1½" H to 3" V/8" H.
   b. Type the text "Aztec Film Society" and update the display.
   c. Change the font to Imprint MT Shadow.
   d. Change the shape to Deflate (Bottom): fifth row, fourth from the left.
   e. Click the Expand to Frame button (to the left of the Center Align button).
   f. Click the workspace to return to the publication.
   g. Save your work.

4. **Create a bleed.**
   a. Create a banner custom shape—using the second custom shape from the left in the sixth row—on the scratch area from 1½" V/-4½" H to 3" V/0" H.
   b. Change the fill color of the shape to black.
   c. Rotate the object counterclockwise 35 degrees.
   d. Move the box so the top edge of the shape is at -½" V/3" H. The banner will span the top-left corner of the page at a 35-degree angle.
   e. Save the publication.

5. **Create a watermark.**
   a. Change to the background view.
   b. Select the film reel clip art on the scratch area.
   c. Resize the image on the right scratch area—while maintaining its scale—so that the shape's top-right corner is at 1" V/14¾" H.
   d. Move the image so that its top-left corner is at 1" V/1½" H.
   e. Recolor the image using the Lilac color box.
   f. Change to the foreground view.
   g. Save the publication.

6. Wrap text around a frame.
   a. Select the image on the left scratch area.
   b. Drag the image so that its top-left edge is at 5½" V/6" H and send the image to the front.
   c. Rotate the image clockwise to a 350-degree angle.
   d. Resize the image to scale so that its top-left edge is at 5¾" H.
   e. Wrap the text to the picture.
   f. Save the publication.

7. Rotate a text frame.
   a. Draw a new text frame from 4" V/9" H to 4¾" V/14" H.
   b. Change the font to 48 point Imprint MT Shadow.
   c. Type "Help us succeed!" in the text frame.
   d. Change the font color to lilac and the fill color to black.
   e. Rotate the text frame 90 degrees.
   f. Move the text frame so that the top-left edge is at 1½" V/7¼" H.
   g. Save your work.
   h. Print the publication.

8. Create a Web page.
   a. Create a Web page from this current publication.
   b. Run the Design Checker and check all the pages.
   c. Ignore the text frame overflow text problem, then close the Design Checker.
   d. Preview the Web site.
   e. Close the browser.
   f. Close the unsaved publication without saving the document.
   g. Exit Publisher.

▶ Independent Challenges

1. The Floral Delights Flower Shop has asked you to create an Open for Business door sign. It would like the sign to include the name of the shop in a curved design that can later be used as a logo.
   To complete this independent challenge:

   a. Start Publisher if necessary.
   b. Open the file PUB G-3 and save it as Floral Delights sign on your Project Disk.
   c. Add BorderArt to the existing frame surrounding the page.
   d. Add WordArt containing the shop's name. (*Hint:* you can resize and move the existing text "Open" if necessary.)
   e. Select clip art that you will use as a watermark. The watermark should appear in the background view in any color you choose.
   f. Move and rotate any objects on the page.
   g. Use the spelling checker and Design Checker when finished.
   h. Save the publication.
   i. Print the publication.

2. The Books and More bookstore has asked you to design a new business card. This business card should have a new logo that includes the store's name. You should also include a graphic image that appears to have text wrapping to the frame.

To complete this independent challenge:

a. Start Publisher if necessary.

b. Open the file PUB G-4 and save it as Books and More card on your Project Disk.

c. Replace the "your name" text with your own name.

d. Add BorderArt to the perimeter of the card.

e. Design a logo using WordArt, and place it on the card.

f. Move any objects on the card to suit your design.

g. Add a graphic image to the card, then make text wrap around it.

h. Resize the image to best fit the publication.

i. Use the Design Checker and spelling checker and make any necessary adjustments.

j. Save the publication.

k. Print the publication.

3. You've decided that your computer consulting firm, The Byte Bucket, needs a new image, so you're redesigning your business cards. Later, you'll use elements from this business card on your letterhead and other print materials.

To complete this independent challenge:

a. Start Publisher if necessary.

b. Use the Business Card Catalog to create a new business card.

c. Save the publication on your Project Disk as Byte Bucket card.

d. Add your name and pertinent information you choose.

e. Use WordArt to design a logo that includes the company's name.

f. Use BorderArt on the perimeter of the card.

g. Add a graphic image—as a watermark—that displays in the background.

h. Arrange the information in an attractive format, using your graphics skills.

i. Create a bleed for one edge of the card.

j. Save and print the publication.

WEB WORK

4. Your hometown library has asked you to create a home page on the World Wide Web. In preparation, you've looked at home pages for other libraries. Using your Publisher skills, you want to create a fancy page for your library.

To complete this independent challenge:

a. Log on to the Internet and use your browser to go to http://www.course.com. From there, click the link Student Online Companions, then click the Microsoft Publisher 98—Illustrated Introductory.

b. Use each of the sites as examples of the types of information in a library site.

c. Find one or two other Web sites for nearby libraries.

d. Start Publisher if necessary.

e. Use the Catalog to create a Web site called Library home page.

f. Save the file as Library home page on your Project Disk.

g. Create a logo for the library using WordArt.

h. Add BorderArt to call attention to a shape within the page.

i. Replace heading placeholders with your own headings.

j. Use the Design Checker and spelling checker to verify accuracy.

k. Save the publication.

l. Publish the Web site on your Project Disk.

m. Print the publication.

Visual Workshop

Open the file PUB G-5 and save it on your Project Disk as Pam's Pet Shop business card. Create a text frame for the company name, then rotate it. This rotated text frame makes use of the Rockwell Extra Bold 14 point font. Use the image on the scratch area to create the watermark (using the gray color box). Use Figure G-28 as a guide. Save and print the publication.

FIGURE G-28

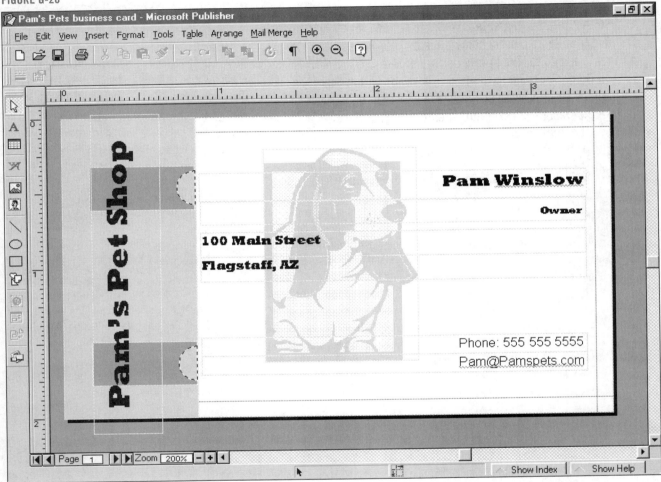

Glossary

Align To line up objects using the top, bottom, center, left, or right edges.

Autoflow Feature that automatically places text not fitting within a text frame into the next available text frames.

Background Behind-the-scenes area of a page used for repetitive objects or text.

Bleed An object that extends beyond a printer's print area that can be trimmed later.

Booklet A publication containing a series of folds or binds.

BorderArt Decorative borders that come with Publisher (or can be created) and can be placed around a frame or box.

Bulleted list Used to illustrate items that can occur in any order.

Catalog Helps create different types of publications.

Clip art Electronic artwork available on your computer.

Clipboard Temporary holding area in Windows that can be used to hold data for later use.

Clip Gallery Live Microsoft's Web site that continually offers new downloadable images.

Clip Gallery Online artwork organizer in Publisher.

Continued on/Continued from notices Text that automatically tells you where a story is continued on or continued from.

Copyfitting Makes the copy fit the space within a publication.

Crop Conceals portions of an image.

Design Gallery Formatted elements—such as pull quotes, sidebars, and titles—that can be added to an existing publication.

Design Sets Groups of matching elements in the Design Gallery that contain common themes, colors, or objects.

Desktop publishing program A program that lets you manipulate text and graphics to create a variety of publication documents.

Dot leaders Tiny dots or dashes that make it easier to read a table of contents or other information.

Drawing tools Toolbox buttons that let you create geometric designs.

Drop caps A formatting feature that lets you change the appearance of a paragraph's initial character.

Flip Objects created using drawing tools which can be rotated horizontally or vertically using a toolbar button.

Footer Text that repeats on the bottom of each page.

Foreground Area of a page where most information is placed.

Formatting toolbar Buttons on a toolbar for changing the appearance of objects within a publication.

Frame Object in a publication containing text, a graphic image, a table, or any combination of these.

Graphic image A piece of artwork in electronic form.

Greeked text Appearance of text too small to be legible.

Group Turns multiple objects into a single object.

Grouping Turns several objects into one, which is an easy way to move multiple items.

Handles Small (usually black) squares displayed around the perimeter of a selected object.

Header Text that repeats on the top of each page.

Horizontal ruler Measuring guide that displays above the publication window.

Kerning Adjusts the spacing between character pairs.

Keywords Words used to locate images within the Clip Gallery.

Layer Changes the position of objects in relation to one another so that one appears to be on top (or behind) another.

Layout guides Horizontal and vertical lines on a publication's background and visible on the screen that help you accurately position objects on a page.

Logo Distinctive shape, symbol, or color that is visibly recognized as belonging to a company or product.

Masthead The banner at the beginning of a newsletter that contains its name, volume, issue, and date.

Menu bar Contains menus from which you choose Publisher commands.

Mirrored guides Layout guides and margins on left and right facing pages that appear to be mirror images.

Numbered list Used to list items that occur in a particular sequence.

Object shadow Gives an object the illusion of depth by adding a shadow behind it.

Objects toolbar Contains buttons used to create frames for text, tables, and graphics.

Orientation Position that the paper is printed on.

Point size The measurement of the height of a character. $\frac{1}{72}$nd of an inch equals one point.

Proof print Approximation of how your final printed publication will look.

Publication A document created in Publisher.

Pull quote A short statement extracted from the text and set aside from the body of the text.

Reversed text Formatting method that displays light characters on a dark background.

Rotate Changes the position of an object in degrees (measured from a horizontal plane).

Rotation An object's position measured in degrees from a horizontal plane.

Ruler guides Created in the foreground of individual pages by dragging a ruler while holding [Shift].

Rulers Horizontally and vertically scaled displays beneath the toolbars and to the left of the workspace.

Scanner Hardware that enables you to turn information on a paper copy into an electronic file format.

Scratch area Surrounds the publication page and can be used to store elements.

Sidebar Information not vital to a publication which is placed to the side of the regular text.

Snap To commands When turned on, this feature has a magnetlike effect that pulls whatever is being lined up to the layout guide.

Spelling checker Used to check a story—or the publication—for spelling errors.

Standard toolbar Buttons on a toolbar for completing common tasks, such as saving and printing.

Status bar Located at the bottom of the Publisher window; provides information relevant to the current task.

Story Text in a publication.

Style Defined set of text formatting attributes.

Style by example Names an existing set of text attributes as a style.

Table AutoFormat Pre-existing designs that quickly format a table.

Table Tabular arrangement of information using columns and rows for organization.

Tab A defined location that the insertion point advances to when [Tab] is pressed.

Text frame Graphic object in which text is typed.

Text overflow Text that does not fit within a text frame.

Title bar Displays the program name and the filename of the open publication.

Toolbars Contains buttons for the most frequently used Publisher commands.

Two-Page Spread View that enables you to see two pages at once.

Ungroup Turns a single object into multiple objects.

Ungrouping Turns one combined object into individual objects.

Vertical ruler Measuring guide that displays to the left of the page.

Watermark A faint, lightly shaded image that appears behind other images.

WordArt An object containing curved or wavy text.

Workspace The area where a new or existing publication appears.

Workspace page Contains the currently displayed page.

Zero point The location of zero on both the vertical and horizontal rulers that can be moved; lets you make precise measurements.

Zoom Mode Makes the page scale larger or smaller so you can move in or away from page objects.

Index

Index

Index